"Fantastic tools
and bu
Jason and Cas

THE SPARK TO YOUR SUCCESS

Helping Teens Build Resilience

TEEJAY DOWE

The Spark to Your Success

First published in 2020 by

Panoma Press Ltd
48 St Vincent Drive, St Albans, Herts, AL1 5SJ, UK
info@panomapress.com
www.panomapress.com

Book layout by Neil Coe.

978-1-784529-15-4

The right of TeeJay Dowe to be identified as the author of this work has been asserted in accordance with sections 77 and 78 of the Copyright, Designs and Patents Act 1988.

A CIP catalogue record for this book is available from the British Library.

This book is available online and in bookstores.

Testimonials

"Having worked with TeeJay over the past few years on her Ignition platform, I think *The Spark to Your Success – Helping Teens Build Resilience* offers young people a way to think differently about the choices and options they have when dealing with life's ups and downs while remaining positive throughout!"

Johnathan Joy

"I like the quotes; they are good and inspirational. I can now go up the stairs all by myself like a big boy; this is because I was scared of the monsters, but now I can go upstairs with confidence knowing that GiGi and Ellie will have fought all the monsters away."

Regan

"We decided to sit down together as a family to discuss the chapters we had individually read. This helped us in so many ways; it has been a whole learning experience we can all participate in and has helped us understand ourselves and each other so much more. The book is super-easy to digest, with bite-size, yet hugely powerful chapters and exercises that help you implement them right away. It's a great resource to help teenagers (and their parents) understand how their minds work, why they think what they think, what they can and can't control, and fantastic tools they can use easily to manage negativity and build resilience.

"We wholeheartedly recommend this book for teenagers, for parents and every human being!"

Jason and Cassie

"It's a great book that helps with mindset, really important because if you understand your mindset, you can understand everyone else's."

Kiera

"This book is an absolute must-read for all teens who want to live a happier and more fulfilling life. TeeJay breaks down how our minds work, how we process information, and how we can build resilience and choose our emotions at any time, giving life-changing tips for people of any age!"

Summer Rose

Acknowledgements

Life is a series of adventures, surprises and unexpected diversions: twists and turns along the way that lead you to the most wonderful people and places. *The Spark to Your Success* has been just one of those journeys and this one started in December 2018 when someone said, "You should start a podcast!"

"Podcast?" I thought. "That would be wonderful, except that I have no clue how to do the technical bits."

Ta-dah! Enter Charlotte Foster of Charlotte Foster Podcasts who, over a cuppa and a lot of glitter, persuaded me that if I did my stuff, she would do hers and get my show on the road, or rather, on air. And so *The Spark to Your Success* podcast began on the first week of January 2019 and has broadcast every week since then. My thanks to you, Charlotte Foster, for making it easy to get my messages out to the young and young at heart, without which the transcripts of the episodes would not have turned into the magic of this book (and the books to come).

That leads me nicely on to say a HUGE thank you to the very gifted, talented and all-round wonderful person that is Anna Woolliscroft. Anna took my ramblings and turned them into blogs, then worked her magic to bring the blogs together into themes and finally into the chapters of this book. Without her, this book would still be an idea waiting to happen for many months (or years) to come.

Once the words were flowing, I needed someone to bring the subjects to life with humour and pictures. There was only one man for the job: Simon Chubb of Scartoons. Thank you, Simon, for making me smile with your quirky cartoons that so beautifully depict my themes.

Finally, thank you to all the people who have touched my life in a way that has left a positive impact – a lesson, a blessing, an inspiration, a truth and many magical moments to be grateful for.

Let's continue to shine our lights into the world and be the Spark to Success!

Contents

Chapter 1
Introduction

As a teenager or young person at heart you face many challenges. Unfortunately, these challenges don't single you out and teen problems won't affect only you. They have affected many before you and will affect many after you.

"There are two great days in a person's life — the day we are born and the day we discover why."

William Barclay

There are two things to be sure of in life:

- Crap will hit the fan at some point (maybe even more than once)

- You have a choice about how to react to the crap aftermath

At this point, let me throw in a nugget of wisdom as a third point to think about. If your choice is well thought out with a positive approach, you will quickly overcome obstacles in your path and build resilience to tackle future challenges.

Understand one thing. It's you who's in the driving seat of your life. You will have opportunities and you will have obstacles. How to face the positive and negative events in your life is down to you. *You have a choice.* You will need to think for yourself and accept the outcome whether it's good or bad.

It's your responsibility, not that of your parents, or your teachers, or your friends or your siblings. *It's up to you.*

OK, pep talk over. This book is split into three main sections:

- An exploration into teen issues and some of the reasons why you encounter them

- A deep dive into what's going on in your head – potentially right now – and how to build resilience

- Finding your fuel and your flow and what works for you to become magnificent

The book is serious with some powerful techniques to make you feel awesome, but you need to understand that *the awesomeness resides inside you already*. It just needs awakening.

I can hear the worriers thinking, "How the *&£$ will I know what to do?"

"I'm struggling; that's why I've got this book."

"I don't know where to start."

"Where is this awesomeness because it's done sweet FA so far!"

Fear not. That's what I'm here for. My purpose in life is to empower 10 million young people to become tomorrow's confident, successful leaders, who do it by feeling happy in their own skin. I've already helped thousands of young people to find their identity, raise their heads above obstacles and find happiness in life.

Let's get back on track to *uncover the spark to your success and start your journey to feeling magnificent.*

It'll be a discovery

This book will introduce you to ways that will help you overcome challenges and grab opportunities when they present themselves. It will equip you with the skills and thought processes to become RESILIENT, CONFIDENT and POSITIVE. Throughout your discovery you will relate to some of the situations we discuss. Some events may trigger happy or unhappy memories, and either is OK. There is no right or wrong way to find yourself. But remember: you have a choice about whether you hold on to bad memories, and I strongly recommend that you accept that %£@! happens and just let it go. *You cannot change the past or predict the future.*

There may be a few bumps along the road

It won't be an easy journey to become magnificent. Do you know why? Because life *isn't* easy. Life requires you to be an active participant in its journey. You will need to think for yourself and complete the exercises illustrated in this book to become a stronger, more positive individual. To become magnificent, you cannot immerse yourself in a virtual reality world – gaming, social media and bingeing on endless box sets. You cannot shut out the real world and still find your awesomeness.

This book will not dissect the issues you face as a teenager. It will not dwell on damaging labels so easily dished out to people. And it will not allow you to wallow in negativity. *This book is for teenagers who want to enjoy life to its absolute fullest.* Sure, you might be going through a few ups and downs – who doesn't? If life were easy, there would be no war, no famine, no poverty and no climate catastrophe.

You'll be an active learner

At certain points in the book I will prompt you to carry out an exercise or make a few notes about your immediate thoughts. This is important because it will allow you to reflect on why you react as you do. I will also prompt you to write out certain sentences or keywords. Sentences will be in italics and keywords will be highlighted in CAPITALS. There will also be a few definitions of words and phrases that you may not have seen or heard of before. The definition will appear in a way that is similar to how it would appear in a dictionary.

You'll see some icons (weird little images in the margin) that will pop up now and again to indicate an exercise, definition or PDF resource. Try to get used to what each icon means, so that you know what's coming next.

All these details will form a summary of the book in your own words to refer to as and when you choose.

Never dwell on the past

Many issues that cause you grief today happened in the past. Unless you can find a time machine to scoot back and reset the situation, it's already happened. You can do absolutely nothing to change the outcome. Choose to accept it and move on. *Never waste your energy on something you can't change.*

Build your shield

You can build your own armour for the real world, to go out there and enjoy every second. I'm going to help you to find your uniqueness and define your purpose.

Think about your favourite character from a Marvel or DC comic. Each character has their uniqueness and superpower. What makes your favourite character different? If you could choose a superpower, what would it be?

Would it surprise you if I were to say that you don't actually need a superpower to be unique and magnificent? Well you don't. *You just need to be you and to be comfortable in your own skin.* Sometimes though, you may need a little help to get there. And that's OK. There's nothing defeatist or weak about getting support. In fact, it's a victory to ask for help.

When you feel comfortable in your own skin and enjoy life, *you have found your identity and true purpose.* You have found your FLOW and your FUEL.

Back on track

The Spark to Your Success: Helping Teens Build Resilience is the first book in a series of *The Spark to Your Success* resources. Each chapter will take between 5 and 10 minutes to read, plus your time to reflect and carry out any exercises outlined. I suggest you complete each exercise before moving on to the next chapter, to help gel your learning.

Still with me? Are you motivated? Cool. Let's get started.

Here are things you'll need:

- A pen or pencil

- A notebook or journal

- Some scrap paper or Post-it notes for scribbling notes

- A highlighter

- Access to your photographs and a camera.

Notice that I've not mentioned making notes on an electronic device. This is on purpose because physical handwriting is important for brain development and thinking capacity. Handwriting is personal and will allow you to connect better with your activity. It also forces you to slow down and think more by engaging extra parts of the brain. Ditch the mobile or laptop and reconnect with the ancient art of putting pen to paper!

"We are what we repeatedly do. Excellence, then, is not an act, but a habit."

Aristotle

Chapter 2

Live life so it rocks!

First, I'd like to start off with a short story about life that I think you'll relate to. Even at your tender age. It's a powerful story because it illustrates so well the pressure of life and how, before you know it, you can become bogged down with unnecessary stuff – emotional and physical.

This is a story about rocks.

A walk in the park

I recently took a trip to the local park to collect rocks for my local youth club in preparation for a creative painting session. My backpack was light, and I had all the time in the world. The morning was beautiful with the sun gazing down on me as the birds tweeted in the trees.

I was looking for a specific size of rock, but as I pottered around grassy pathways, my mind wandering, I started to pick up small pebbles. They weren't exactly what I was after, but I thought they might come in handy if I couldn't find my ideal rock, so in the backpack they went.

Deviating off track

At some point during my ramble – I have no idea when – I'd gone off track and now stood in a glorious glade full of stunningly colourful flowers. The scene was fabulous, very inspiring, but I had no idea how I had got there or how much time I'd lost. I breathed in the sweet air for a moment then backtracked until I found my original pathway. By this time, I could feel the strain of my backpack and a dull ache making its presence known on my shoulder.

Within a few minutes, I turned a corner and woohoo! There lay a jackpot of rocky rubble ahead. I bounded over excitedly and crammed half a dozen rocks into my backpack. If I'm honest, a couple were too big, but I bagged them anyway before moving on.

My backpack was now getting really heavy and I felt hot and bothered. It weighed a ton and I could have done with offloading a few rocks that weren't ideal, but I thought they might still come in handy for the future so held on to them. The hefty weight was stretching the backpack handles and my back was also starting to hurt.

A great metaphor for life

You might be wondering why I'm telling you a story about carrying rocks. Well, it's a great metaphor for life. Simple.

When you start off on a journey, everything is as light as a feather and you feel fabulous because you have a PURPOSE. Then you get sidetracked and start to pick up baggage that you don't really need, but you think might come in handy somewhere. This adds extra and often unnecessary pressure in some areas of your life – both mental and physical – yet you continue your journey unwittingly (or wittingly), knowing that these pressures can be damaging.

What unnecessary baggage are you carrying?

Think about this question and this story as you delve deeper into the book. Take a long look at your life as it stands today.

- What are you doing, saying or feeling that you don't really need to be doing, saying or feeling?

- What would happen if you stopped and offloaded this extra stuff that is weighing you down?

You might have a couple of peers that you would rather not have in your life. Maybe you go to an after-school class that you don't really enjoy, but you do it to please your parents. It could just be that you are a people-pleaser and you don't like to let people down, so you have a full calendar of outings because you struggle to say no, when all you really want to do is curl up in the privacy of your own room with a good book.

If you got rid of these additional burdens, think how much lighter you would feel. Imagine the extra room you would have created in your life to do the things that bring you more value and enjoyment.

Everyone falls victim to this but *recognising the signs so that you can make the change is key*. Draw up a list of things that you feel hold you back or drag you back, and think about how you can offload them.

Unload, repack and carry on

This book will give you tools to lighten your load, to plan and to work smarter not harder. It will introduce you to ways of creating an agile and stress-free life by equipping you with the techniques needed to overcome carrying unnecessary rocks because of the fear of missing out. If you feel fulfilled, you'll never miss out on anything.

Try painting rocks

Oh, and I recommend that you try painting rocks. It's hugely therapeutic and extremely creative. Find a few big pebbles, some acrylic paints, and Google ideas for rock painting designs. You will find tons of really cool pictures of quirky images, animals, patterns and written messages.

If you enjoy it, why not paint more than you want for yourself and leave them in your village, town or the local park for other people to discover and enjoy. Tracking painted rocks actually is a thing you know!

Share your journey with others

What I would love more than anything is for you to share your thoughts and stories as you read this book. We all want to help each other and feel supported along the way. You can learn from others and combine experiences so that the tools and techniques develop further.

Please do share your feelings on social media:

- www.instagram.com/ignition.rocks
- www.facebook.com/IgnitionYP
- www.twitter.com/ignition2017

And if you feel as though you need any extra help at any time, message me directly on my personal email: teejay@backontrackteens.com

OK, let's begin…

Chapter 3

Pressures of a typical teen life

"You were given this life because you are strong enough to live it."

Ain Eineziz

Obstacles litter your path every day, and I'm not talking about inconsiderate people chucking crisp packets and pop bottles on the floor. The obstacles I'm talking about are life hurdles. They cause setbacks, create problems and present new questions to think about. They are a pain in the backside, and they add pressure that you can do without.

Boom! That's life, right there!

You're the only one that has problems

Hmm... you might think that, but everyone has challenges to overcome and everyone feels pressure. If you find someone who says not, I promise you, they are lying and just trying to save face.

Feeling pressure as a teenager can be overwhelming because you are encountering many problems for the first time. This adds fear and uncertainty because the future is unknown. To make matters worse, for you as a teenager growing up in the 2020s, the everyday pressures from teachers, parents, friends, siblings and employers are compounded by the pressures of the online world and uber-connectedness. *I praise your generation, honestly.* Mobile phones weren't a commodity when I was a wee lass.

Every teen has pressure in their life. Past experiences, fears about the future, aspirations and how you choose to handle a situation will determine the extent of the pressure you feel. Throughout this book you will be introduced to proven techniques to help you cope with pressure and live life to the absolute max.

In fact, you are probably doing far better than you think you are, so give yourself some credit.

Standing up in front of everyone at school

Does the thought of this freak you out?

You're sitting in class, feeling somewhat uncomfortable. One of your legs is juddering uncontrollably, you feel hot and sweaty and your tummy is churning. You are supposed to be listening to your fellow students as they each present their viewpoint on a question asked by the teacher last week, but all you can think about is the ways in which your own presentation could go wrong:

- What if you forget your words?

- What if you start to stammer?

- What if the class bully picks up on something and makes your life hell on the way home?

This might not be the exact situation that gives you the heebie-jeebies, but it's a pressure that many teenagers have sleepless nights over.

Typical teenage problems relate to body image and identity. It's a period in life where you are experiencing massive body and emotional changes. You are trying to find yourself, and some situations may make you feel vulnerable. You may also compare yourself to others (we'll come to this later in the book, but just know that there's no need for you to do this).

Think carefully. When was the last time something got on top of you? It may have been the classroom presentation mentioned above, maybe an exam, a job interview, a sports competition, or a massive bust-up with your parents, sibling or a friend (or a not-so-nice non-friend at school).

How did this situation or person make you feel?

Pay attention to how you feel

It's natural to feel something. Feeling nothing doesn't make you the cool kid. Quite the opposite. Feeling intense negative reactions and surviving them helps you to learn valuable lessons, gain new skills and develop the ability to adapt. Fist bump to you! But what can you expect to feel when pressure raises its head? (By the way, it's not always an ugly head.)

When stuff gets on top of you, you can feel:

- Fearful
- Sad
- Angry

- Anxious

- Pain

- Disappointed

Negative emotions can cause you to make snap decisions or take hasty action. This happens because you haven't taken time to think about the situation before responding and the chances are that it might not be the right response. But that's OK. How you react to obstacles and pressure helps you to learn better coping techniques. It helps you to become more confident, tougher and happier. *This is where the magic lies.*

Butterflies, breakouts and bad moods

Feeling pressure can manifest as anything from belly butterflies to feeling absolutely paralysed by your thoughts. Have you ever felt as though your head is pounding, your stomach is churning, and you can't get to sleep at night?

This is your sign.

Have you ever felt that your heart is racing? A sudden hot flush takes over you. Do you ever want to cry or shout or lock yourself in your bedroom so that everything will disappear?

This is normal but remember that these signs are short-term responses to pressure. Scientifically this is called the fight-or-flight response.

https://en.wikipedia.org/wiki/Fight-or-flight_response

Stuff happens to your body and in your mind when you're fearful. You believe that whatever is happening is beyond your control and consequently your body is preparing to run away or stand tall and raise fists. It's the same for pressure. Standing up to pressure and dealing with the situation is where you want to be. *Running away is not the solution.* Neither is a fistfight in most situations.

Get off the pressure train

The feeling of being under constant pressure can build up to the point that you feel like a bottle of pop ready to burst. But let's not get to burst point. What you don't want is to feel the effects of long-term pressure:

- Meltdowns
- High anxiety
- Depression
- Low self-esteem
- Breakdowns
- Suicidal thoughts

There are some physical changes to be aware of too:

- Continuous and severe breakouts
- Dark circles under your eyes
- Weight gain
- Weight loss

- Blood pressure fluctuations

- Shaking limbs

- Headaches or migraines

- Stomach upsets, pains and bloating

These physical ailments are also linked to your general wellbeing, diet and exercise. When you are worried, stressed or angry (to name but a few), it can affect your appetite. Bad food and drink choices will compound the effects of feeling pressure.

Remember, you can handle life and you can handle it well.

Coping with teen pressures – you've got this

When you feel under pressure, take a deep breath and take your time to consider the situation. Is it the end of the world? Probably not, so work out how best to react by weighing up a few options:

- What's the worst that could happen?

- What's the best that could happen?

Find a balance that's right because *overthinking situations can cause you to make no decision at all!*

It helps if you can speak to someone when feeling under pressure. It's not good to hold worries and negative emotions inside, so try to keep kind, supportive and motivational people around you. They will help.

KEEP A JOURNAL. Just to warn you that I'll bang on about this a lot, but please do keep one. They are super-useful to make notes about how you feel and how you overcome obstacles. Your notes will help you to become aware of the positives that work for you and give you time to reflect and work out what you need to do.

Building your armour

Recognise the signs that indicate you are feeling pressure. This is why I'm encouraging you to note memories, motivations and ideas, as well as situations and thoughts that cause you to have negative and positive responses, while you read this book.

Ultimately, there's this neat little skill called RESILIENCE. It's a key factor that will help you to approach and handle obstacles and unexpected situations in your stride and it's a brilliant tool to pick up as a teenager.

"Good habits formed at youth make all the difference."

Aristotle

Chapter 4
Feeling overwhelmed

"Our greatest battles are with our minds."

Jameson Frank

Growing up is a time to find your purpose in life, to discover your identity. Some of the decisions you need to make – such as choosing a career, further education, and defining your own personal beliefs and values – come only from experiencing ups and downs. *Now is a time in your life to ask questions, to be curious* and above all, enjoy yourself.

Feeling overwhelmed happens – rise above it

Feeling overwhelmed can be a regular occurrence, but it's not about having too much homework, a long to-do list or no pocket money. It's way bigger than that.

The dictionary definition of overwhelm: *to bury or drown beneath a huge mass of something, especially water.*

Alternative words: *swamped, submerged, buried, inundated.*

An overwhelming situation is a bit like the flow of uncontrollable floodwater. Nothing can stop it and it's certainly beyond your control.

The second dictionary definition: *to have a strong emotional effect on – "I was overwhelmed with guilt."*

Alternative words: *overcome, dumbfounded, dazed, flawed, staggered.*

These words all describe feelings of being knocked sideways that may lead to confusion, hurt, uncertainty and fear.

Feeling overwhelmed is a state of not knowing which way to turn or what to do first. The situation can feel so big that you may fall into a state of hopelessness where you can feel paralysed. It often feels like the easy option to do nothing. *This is not the best option.*

Feeling out of your depth – step up and step out

Being overwhelmed means a loss of control. Can you think of a time in the past when you felt this way?

Maybe you don't understand a mathematical equation, or you've been given the responsibility to organise a presentation at school and it's way out of your comfort zone because you have to manage other students. What is your experience over the past year, at school, at home or within a social setting, of feeling truly out of your depth?

- What do you think caused this feeling of being overpowered?

- Was it something you did or didn't do?

- Was it something that someone else did or didn't do?

Let's get some perspective on feeling overwhelmed and think about a current situation you are going through.

Consider the following questions about *what is worrying you right now*?

- What is your main bugbear and what are you uncertain of?

- If you could choose to create a positive outcome for this situation, what would it be?

- How would you feel? (Think about your situation as a blockbuster movie and what the happy ending would be.)

- Is the thing you're anxious about in your control? Remember, you cannot control the outside world.

- If the answer is yes, list five ways to make the outcome less scary and unknown.

    o Think about what you need to do to get ready. What do you need to organise or find out?

    o Are there times, routes, or access information you need to source?

If you don't feel ready for something that is about to change or something that you need to do, it's because you don't feel in full control of the situation. *Planning ahead and asking questions about the future will help you to feel more prepared and relaxed, and less overwhelmed.*

When to control the inside not the outside

Despite your best efforts, there will be situations where you cannot completely control the outcome. But you can choose to *control the story you tell yourself, internally*, about the outcome of the situation. Here are a few ways you can do this.

Create five positive new meanings for the situation you feel overwhelmed about. As an example, if you are starting at a new school, college, uni or job:

- Do you feel anxious because you think you won't fit in? Do you worry about no one liking you?

- You may not *fit in*, but you may *stand out* for all the *right* reasons.

- What if you make new friends? What if you find someone who feels the same as you do and so together you both fit in perfectly? If you are ready to learn and grow, you will find your way and won't ever need to worry about not fitting in.

There is a PDF available on the Back on Track Teens website to help with this activity. Please visit:

www.backontrackteens.com/ignition-what-is-worrying-you/

When you feel that it's hard to be superman or superwoman in all things in life

Remember this: you do not need superpowers to be remarkable.

Part of the problem with feeling overwhelmed is how you perceive yourself, but:

- you don't have to be superman or superwomen to feel remarkable and achieve amazing things

- you don't have to be a perfectionist – perfection is a myth

- you don't always have to say yes and be a people pleaser

- you should never overanalyse a situation

Do you recognise yourself in any of the above statements? The first step to overcoming hindering behaviours, a big one of which is feeling overwhelmed, is to *acknowledge them*. Hoorah! Now you know what to do.

I couldn't possibly ask for help

Even though you are learning the skills to stay in control of your emotions and situations, it can help to *ask for support*. There's nothing wrong with asking for help, but you may see it as a sign of weakness. It's not. People love to be asked to help because it makes them feel worthy and wanted.

When you next start to feel overwhelmed, ask yourself, "For this to be done, does it have to be me?"

Think about who else could help. Friends, family, teachers, mentors or trainers? Working with others can make a daunting task appear much easier and perhaps quicker too.

Four fun ways to pull yourself out of an overwhelming situation

When you tackle each task, be *present in the present* and remove all distractions. Choose an environment where you feel comfortable – in the garden, in your bedroom or in a cafe with a view – and take in some deep breaths before you begin. If you can connect with nature, I guarantee you'll feel more grounded.

Take these steps and you will stay in control:

1. Make a task or situation smaller than it is. Pull out the detail and stress of the task by breaking it up into no more than three to five chunks. A good technique is to draw cloud or bucket images on a sheet of paper and in each image write down the big things to do such as research XYZ, speak to XYZ, purchase XYZ – this way you'll see only five things instead of a zillion.

2. Pick one task and work on it for one hour. It's up to you which task you choose first; it can be the most important, the most fun or the easiest – just don't try to multitask.

3. Brainstorm, create a mind map or make lists. Set a timer on your phone for five minutes and brainstorm everything needed for that single task. You don't need to action anything at this stage: just keep writing.

4. Set your alarm for another three minutes and go through your list quickly to sort out an order that feels right to you. Allocate a timeframe to complete the task, then add a few extra minutes, because you will always underestimate the time.

Celebrate each task completion with your favourite snack, a session on the Xbox, a social event with friends, or whatever you feel is a reward for working hard. It's important to look after yourself.

"Nobody is perfect, so stop trying to be perfect."

Lisa Lieberman-Wang

Resources: If you want to explore this concept in more detail, please read my other book, *PerfectShun: Permission to be Human*. It's packed full of insightful information and useful exercises to get stuck into and strengthen your resilience.

Find it here: https://www.ignition.rocks/perfectshun

Chapter 5
Your driving force

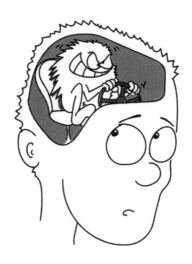

"Having needs is not evidence of weakness — it is human."

Danielle Bernock

I ended the last chapter with a statement about looking after yourself. This leads us nicely into the SIX ESSENTIAL HUMAN NEEDS – *which are your driving force in life.*

Believe it or not, you have six essentials needs to live by. Everybody has them. Everybody needs them. The first four are critical in order to function in life. The final two will allow you to become truly fulfilled in life, but more on that later.

Where did this concept originate?

Several years ago, an American guy called Tony Robbins – www.tonyrobbins.com – came up with a concept that everyone, including you, has six basic human needs.

Tony is a brilliant life coach, business strategist and philanthropist (someone who campaigns for the welfare of others) and over years of research and encountering thousands of people, he noticed that, despite people's differences, including:

- Country of birth and residence
- Culture, beliefs and values
- Language spoken

- Gender identity
- Career path
- Family status

... everyone has the same needs.

Understanding these needs will help you to identify with what makes you, and those around you, tick. *If your needs are met positively and in balance, you're on to a sure thing in life.*

But pay attention! Your behaviours are based on how you meet the six needs. If you fulfil your needs in a negative way, you *will* run the risk of developing poor behaviours that could damage your physical and mental wellbeing. They will also impact those around you.

Why do you do the things you do and what really drives you?

As I explain each need, question what they mean to you and how they make you feel. Are there situations or people that you visualise as your mind tries to make sense of the description?

Need 1: CERTAINTY

Certainty gives you a sense of safety, peace of mind, and a feeling of being in control of your world, inside and out. Certainty is all about knowing what to expect today, tomorrow, next week, and what's coming up in your future life.

Definition: Assurance that you can avoid pain and gain pleasure.

Think back to the last time you felt completely certain about what the outcome of a situation would be.

- Where were you going?

- Who were you meeting?

- What were you about to do?

- Why were you certain of what the outcome would be?

- How did this make you feel?

Can you compare the differences between this situation and the one from the last chapter where you felt completely out of control?

Now think about this from a different point of view: how often do you repeat the exact same process or action? How many times do you always know what to expect? For some people, this creates a comfort zone and takes away the fear of the unknown.

But imagine *this:* every single day you climb out of bed at the same time. You go through the same get-up and get-ready routine. You wear similar clothes every day, eat the same breakfast, take the same journey to school, sit in exactly the same lesson, have the same conversations with the same people, eat an identical lunch and play the same sport in the afternoon.

Then, you take the same journey home in the same vehicle, have exactly the same conversations when you return, eat an identical dinner, watch the same TV programme, read the same book – anybody bored yet?

Life would be pretty dreary if you were certain of everything.

With that in mind, you also have a need for VARIETY.

Need 2: UNCERTAINTY (variety)

Excitement and uncertainty in life is a good thing and looking forward to something new brings a sense of anticipation. How do you feel about surprises or new positive challenges? They feel good – right?

Definition: The need for the unknown, change, an excited sense of anticipation.

When was the last time you really looked forward to an event, a trip or receiving good news, but you weren't quite certain of the outcome?

- What was about to take place?

- Why were you positive about it?

- Who was involved?

Variety is great because you must have change in life to feel excited, challenged and fulfilled. Variation in food, subjects at school, hairstyles, fashion and adventures are all positives.

However, if all things were uncertain, you'd freak out, feel anxious and become stressed. You'd want either to bulldoze your way out of a situation or to lock yourself up in a darkened room to remove the uncertainty.

Picture this: you're not feeling well, so you visit the local surgery. During your appointment, the doctor says, "Hmmm, I don't think it's anything to worry about, but I'll send you to the hospital for some tests just in case." After you've attended the hospital, had the tests and returned home, it's a waiting game until you receive the results.

What happens while you wait? Usually, that little voice inside starts overthinking:

- I wonder what's wrong with me?

- The doctor said it's probably nothing, but he did send me for tests so that means it could be something – right?

- I hope it's not too serious

- I hope I don't have to take medication

- I hope I don't have to take a lot of medication

- If it has some of those awful side effects, I might feel worse than I felt before

- Oh my gosh, I hope I don't have to have an operation

- What if it's a big operation?

- I'll have to have time off school

- I can't have time off school – how will I pass my exams?

- What if it's worse and it's terminal?

- Am I going to die?

- I need the results and then at least I know how to deal with it

Phew, that all sounds very stressful! You made a mountain out of molehill by jumping to all sorts of conclusions when you had zero facts to deal with. When this overthinking and anxiety starts to set in, you need to *get a sense of control back in your life*.

Can you think of a time or situation when there were so many variables in what was happening or about to happen, and you had so many unanswered questions, that the situation had a negative impact on you, when the uncertainty was so high that you were worried or frightened?

Briefly make a note of the situation and the questions you had. Is this situation the same as the one from the chapter 4 exercise where you felt overwhelmed?

Ultimately you need both certainty and uncertainty in your life, but they must be in a balance that's right for you.

Hopefully, you are starting to see the logic in this concept.

"Within the nature of every person
is a desire to feel appreciated,
to feel needed, and to be loved."

Ellen J Barrier

Chapter 6

Your significance and connection

Success and happiness is important in life. Why wouldn't you want to be successful and happy in what you do?

Granted, success and happiness comes in different guises for us all. Part of growing up and experiencing stability and change helps you to find what you thrive (and don't thrive) on.

Certainty and uncertainty can be defined as needs of your personality. So too can the next set of needs. They are also achievement focused.

Need 3: CONNECTION (love)

As a human, you were never meant to be alone.

You are wired for love and connection and the need to be around people.

Definition: A strong feeling of closeness or union with someone or something.

A solitary life is rarely a happy life.

It has been illustrated many times over that not having people and things in your life (to help you to feel happy) affects your mood in a negative way. It's a sad fact that when people feel so unloved and totally alone in the world, believing that no one cares about them, they even take their own lives. This is an extreme example, but very real nonetheless and one that illustrates why these needs are *essential* and not just 'nice things to have' in your life.

Emotional hurt can manifest for many reasons. A lack of love and support from your family or a romantic relationship is common, as is building up a protective wall to prevent yourself from being hurt. Sometimes you might wish to cut all ties for fear of being subjected to that hurtful situation again. But *you still have to connect with people* – even if you are someone who likes your own company or doesn't naturally excel in social gatherings.

Connections can be friends, family, teachers, role models or work colleagues. Positive connections are people with whom you share common likes and interests and it feels good to share similar bonds.

Can you think of a time when you thoroughly enjoyed being with someone or a group of people?

- Who were they?

- What were you doing?

- How did the relationships develop?

- Are you still close to that person or group now?

- What community groups and social media groups are you part of?

- Why do certain topics interest you?

- What is your preferred way to connect with the people involved?

At some point, there will come a time when you feel as though you need your own space – even if you are someone who is naturally the life and soul of a party.

This is because *you are unique and not like anyone else.*

Need 4: SIGNIFICANCE

You are an individual. You have a need to be recognised for your achievements and worth in the world and you have freedom to be able to express yourself too.

Definition: Feeling of being unique, important, special or needed.

There will be times when you will want to take a step back, away from others, to discover your purpose and 'significance' in life. You will need a level of freedom to explore and find your own sense of importance and self-worth.

Discovering your purpose may be through your choice of academic studies or creative exploration. You may be drawn to science, art, politics or the environment. Whatever it is will help you to define your significance compared to others. While I need to stress that it is unhealthy to compare yourself to others (because everyone is unique and magnificent in their own right), you do need a point or points of difference.

Expressing who you are may also be in the way you dress, the way you communicate or the way that you put your thoughts into your art or music or poetry, for example.

As with the need for certainty and uncertainty, you are trying to achieve a balance between the love of connection and the freedom of your individual significance through the ability to express yourself.

If you are too special and too different from anybody else, how are you going to connect with people? Connections work because people like people like themselves. You have things in common and that's how and why you connect.

Think about the last time you felt the need to pull away from a situation or person and be by yourself?

- What caused you to feel this way?

- What did you think was missing from the situation?

- Was there overkill of something?

- Was there more to the situation that you needed to discover but wasn't present at the time?

The first two sets of essential human needs are each a paradox. Too much of one creates an imbalance and you may find difficulty in achieving the other. Spending too much time on nurturing your own significance may cause you to find it challenging to build deep intimate relationships that need love and connection. It's a fine balance.

"Never be bullied into silence. Never allow yourself to be made a victim. Accept no one's definition of your life, but define yourself."

Harvey Fierstein

Chapter 7

Your growth and contribution

The final two needs, which complete the six, can be defined as needs of your spirit rather than needs of your personality.

This is because they are concerned more with the fulfilment of your life and not just the essentials needed to exist. They give you a reason to live and a desire to give back.

Need 5: GROWTH

You may find it hard to believe if you can't stand being at school or hate the subjects you're studying, but you have a built-in need to LEARN. Honestly ☺.

Definition: An expansion of capacity, capability or understanding.

Forget school or college for a moment and think about what excites you. What's your CURIOSITY? You choose specific book topics to read, movies to watch, music or podcasts to listen to, games to play or websites and interest groups to review. You choose them because the theme or activity excites you and you want to know more. You want to immerse yourself in the nitty gritty of it all and soak up every last detail.

This is how you *grow as a person, gain new knowledge, improve skills and develop interest*. If you did not learn and grow, what would happen? You'd wilt away to nothing, that's what. Plus it wouldn't matter how many friends you had, how good your grades were or how much money you earned, if you didn't enjoy life and live it to your max. Legally I must add!

The growth of a relationship, a career, a business, your knowledge, your thirst for adventure and experience must be met. For your mind to grow, you must *stretch yourself by learning and growing constantly*. Every day is an education day, even after you finish compulsory education.

What was the last thing that you did or learned that you truly enjoyed?

- What gave you that buzz?

- Can you think of a reason why?

- When did you do something to help someone else, a cause or a group?

- How did it make you feel?

- Why did you choose to do it?

Alongside your need to grow, you also have a need to 'contribute'.

Need 6: CONTRIBUTION

Contributing is doing something that isn't always for your own personal or best interest: giving something away, in time, money, effort or skills. Examples include volunteering at the local dog rescue centre, helping the elderly with household chores or donating a monthly amount to your favourite charity.

Definition: A sense of service and focus on helping, giving to and supporting others.

Contribution is your way of giving something back, of spreading an ACT OF KINDNESS and of feeling content about a good deed.

This concept of contribution is important when you want to influence the people around you. If you say or do positive things, if you listen to and appreciate the thoughts and needs of friends and family (and acquaintances), they will feel valued. This is also a valid way to meet some of your own needs. The difference though is that rather than you simply meeting a need, you are fulfilling the other person's needs as well as your own to the point that they are overflowing. Hoorah!

You are living life to the full and the needs of growth and contribution are serving you well. High five to you!

Can you think of a time recently when you went out of your way to help someone? Maybe it was another person – a stranger, a sibling, a friend, a family member, an animal in need, or perhaps a charitable campaign or community cause.

- What elements attracted you to help?

- Who was involved?

- How did you help?

- Did you give away your time, skills or money, or did you just listen?

- What was the outcome?

- What opportunities did this lead to for you?

- Have you done this more than once?

It feels good to grow and contribute, but you can achieve this effectively only if the other four needs of your personality are in balance first.

You cannot give away too much or take too much without it upsetting the balance. Too much of one can cause upset, emotional turmoil and affect how you enjoy life.

Stretch yourself

Between now and next week, I want to challenge you do a little research and find a new area of interest that you would like to learn more about. This could be an outdoor activity, a short online course or a local social group that meets weekly. In addition, find a way that you can contribute to a local community group or charity, or just some way of giving something back without wanting anything in exchange. This could be as simple as helping a younger sibling with their homework. Journal what you do and how it makes you feel. I'm sure it'll be very rewarding.

Let's draw a line under what the six human needs are and review the negative behaviours that can arise from your needs not being met in a positive way. It happens and it's OK, as long as you can *recognise why this happens* and can *alter your behaviours.*

Please share your outcome with us on social media.

- www.instagram.com/ignition.rocks
- www.facebook.com/IgnitionYP
- www.twitter.com/ignition2017

Chapter 8

Negative behaviours if needs aren't being met

"Life is full of surprises. Not all these surprises are pleasant, so you need to be ready for what life brings you."

Unknown

Awesome. You now know what attributes are needed to lead a balanced and enjoyable life. Onwards and upwards! Why is it then that people find it so easy to slip into meeting their needs by adopting negative behaviours?

Fast food is more convenient – developing negative behaviours

Not everyone values the six needs equally. One or two needs will always take priority and drive how you lead your life. The way in which you meet your needs might be different from the way your friend achieves the same needs.

Let me explain by giving the example of fast food. A 'certain' thing in life is that you need food to survive. You might meet this need by whipping up a MasterChef culinary delight every night (or Mum or Dad will), but how much easier would it be to pull up at a fast-food drive-thru? It might be illogical to you, but this might be exactly what your BFF would do.

At a fast-food drive-thru, the food is ordered and handed straight to you through a window – almost immediately.

You waste no time plodding along supermarket aisles or rummaging through kitchen cupboards and the fridge for multiple ingredients to make a mouth-watering meal. And that's before you peel, chop, cook and serve. Microwave or oven meals are easy to cook, but there's no real preparation involved. It's instant. You don't even need a plate.

This is all true and you can't argue with the facts. But what I would argue is that a fast-food diet or one that doesn't include freshly prepared food and a variety of nutritional ingredients is far less healthy. There tends to be more sugar and fat in convenience foods to make them taste better and to prolong their shelf life.

More calories + less nutrition = no fuel for a healthy body

We'll discuss healthy eating later and I'll provide you with some useful tips, but for now, I hope you get the gist that a little effort brings a better outcome or at least a healthier outcome.

Undervaluing your needs

Eating fast or convenience food in the long term is a negative behaviour.

While it does meet the 'certainty' need that you are fed and fuelled to live another day, it suggests that you undervalue the need for health and wellbeing. Lack of nutrition, key vitamins and variety across the main food groups can lead to deficiencies and affect your body's immune system.

Yet slipping into negative behaviours such as overly eating convenience foods happens because they often appear to be the easier option.

Yes, but I need this!

Overvaluing your needs is a dangerous game.

There will be times when a need is overvalued because it makes you feel better and therefore is the most desirable. A prime example to think about is the need for CONNECTION (love).

If you feel ill or come across an obstacle that you can't control the outcome of, you may feel down or be restricted in some way from doing what you would normally do. In such situations, if you share your experience, perhaps by posting how you feel on social media, you may be showered with affection and gain extra attention from your friends and family. This extra attention will make you feel special. Of course it will – even if you felt bad in the first place.

You feel *significant* because you are the centre of attention. Your needs are being met because you are 'connecting' with people and, on some level, you also meet the need for 'certainty'. You're sure that people will mollycoddle you because they have done so before.

You'll even have a dose of 'variety' to bring excitement to the equation. If you've been ill, you may receive loving messages, cards and flowers, or time off school or work. But do you really want to be ill continually, just to gain the attention of others? It's not a healthy long-term strategy, is it? It's this type of behaviour that can lead to substance misuse through the perceived high it brings or the cover-up effect it offers against the void of unfulfilled needs.

The behaviour battle

The battle between positive and negative behaviours happens in your nervous system as an unconscious process. It is in your UNCONSCIOUS MIND that negative behaviours develop. If you talk to yourself often enough using unhelpful language such as *I can't*, *I won't*, or *it's too difficult*, your mind will try to find the easiest way to meet your needs. Unfortunately, this could be in a negative way.

It helps to consider things, situations or relationships on a scale of 1 to 10. If you score a 10, amazing: that part of your life is sweet. If you score around 4 to 6, you're not exactly happy but you're probably happy enough not to force a change. If a three or below springs to mind, life is pretty dull and you're more likely to consciously make a change. Make sense?

This is especially true when you feel down and is why it's so important to spot the signs and use techniques to lift spirits.

Have you ever felt really low for a sustained period of time?

- What behaviours did you develop?

- How did you feel?

- What happened to make you feel this way?

- Which of the six needs did you meet?

- How did you overcome this dark period?

Beware or be aware of negative behaviours

Getting stuck in a negative behaviour can be beneficial in the short term because you'll no doubt learn a lesson or progress in a different, more positive direction. But getting stuck in prolonged negative behaviours becomes addictive and can lead to:

- Overeating

- Overspending

- Excessive drinking

- Taking drugs

- Violence or seeking conflict

- Craving attention – sexual or otherwise

Succumbing to anxiety, depression or anorexia, for example, or turning to substance abuse or antisocial behaviour are also ways to meet your needs. But these are far from positive, aren't they?

It may seem illogical, but when the behaviour meets many needs at a high level at the same time you will sacrifice your standards to keep meeting your needs. If it becomes habit, it will become more difficult to change. Developing resilience to events that can lead to negative behaviour is the answer. You can *achieve this by staying positive, building your confidence and being magnificent.* You'll learn more about how to do this later in this book.

Who is more at risk from negative behaviours?

The short answer is everyone. Yes, everyone is at risk from developing negative behaviours – even if they feel positive and balanced. We all have to meet our needs.

Think about a long-distance runner or gym fanatic – this could be you. You may think that exercise and body conditioning are positive behaviours, and they are, but *addiction can arise from a need being met on a high level.* In this example, the need to stay fit becomes an obsession, so you work out or run every day and probably increase exertion too. At some point, your body will start to show signs of wear and tear. Energy reserves and nutrients will divert from looking after your entire body, to serve only the organs and limbs needed to work out. Do you see where this could lead?

- Injury
- Distancing
- Alienation
- Performance high over enjoyment

Even positive behaviours can turn addictive and therefore negative. When this happens, it's not that you are a bad person, more a case that you are using poor behaviours to meet a need that is overvalued or undervalued.

Think about the situations below. What needs do you believe would be met if:

- You knew you could earn more money for the next six months?

- You had a set routine every day for the next week?

- A classmate threw a bottle of water across the room?

- A friend always had a date to go on each weekend?

- You were awarded an achievement certificate?

- A friend got an outrageous piercing?

- A classmate started to become a bully?

Which of these needs are positive and which are negative? If you feel some of them are negative, what would be a different and positive reaction to a similar situation? I'll reveal the answers to this at some point later in the book.

Remember, people are not their behaviours. The behaviour is an outward symptom of an unmet need. Love the person – change the behaviour.

"Life is full of unexpected things but always remember that it's hard to beat a person who never gives up."

Smrutishreee Avinash

Chapter 9

Your daily 60,000 thoughts

The last few chapters have introduced you to the key needs in life and the potential bad stuff that could happen if the needs scale is unbalanced. Now it's time to share the really good stuff so that you know how to keep the balance in favour of the positive.

Developing an all-time high?

If words were a pick-me-up, this is the point at which you would be legally allowed to embrace an eternal high. I'll let you into a secret. It's all about *how you interpret what happens in the external world, in your internal world,* also known as your mind.

Would it shock you to learn that you have around 60,000 THOUGHTS every single day? And every day you are having pretty much the same 60,000 thoughts over and over. If the constant chatter inside your head is always negative it can be lethal, so learning how to keep your negative voice at bay will make you more RESILIENT (and a more enjoyable person to be around).

When do these 60,000 thoughts happen?

Good question. The answer is constantly. Sometimes the thoughts are loud enough for you to hear and notice. Sometimes they are too loud and feel like they are shouting at you. And all too often they quietly whisper in the background, so quietly that you hardly hear them, but they can still influence you.

When an event (a situation or action) occurs in the world, whether it's your immediate world or the wider world, it happens as an outside event – away from your inner thoughts. This could be an argument at home, an incident with your mates at the park or an event in the classroom. Whatever this event is, it did not originate from your brain. It's in your outside world and it's just an event. From your point of view, at the very start of an event, you have not yet assigned a meaning and there is no emotional feeling or physical reaction to it.

As an event unfolds, you take the outside information into your mind through your senses of sight, sound, touch, taste or smell. Only then can a meaning be assigned, and it all happens in a matter of milliseconds.

What causes so many thoughts?

Life! Experiences! Encounters!

Contrary to what your parents or teachers might tell you, there is a whole lot more than empty space between your two ears. Your brain is remarkable. That grey matter with its 84 billion nerve cells processes millions of pieces of information every second, no matter how old you are.

At this point I'd like to introduce you to 'Bob' – he's available to download here, to keep with you at all times: www.backontrackteens.com/wp-content/uploads/2019/11/Ignition-Bob.pdf

Bob is perfect if you're a visual learner, but he will also help you to make sense of this subject in a playful way, even if you're an auditory or kinaesthetic learner.

I'll add an explanation here to illustrate that you have a preferred learning style: visual, auditory or kinaesthetic. The first two styles should be obvious, but the last is concerned more with 'somatic' feelings, such as pressure and temperature as well as emotions. Bob mentions this concept as 'VAKOG', which includes olfactory and gustatory styles, that is, relating to smell and taste. Keep these elements in mind when you learn anything new and seek teaching methods more likely to help you absorb the information.

If you're an auditory learner, this podcast will be a good place for you to dip into: https://shows.acast.com/sparktoyoursuccess/episodes/resilient-thinking.

And for everyone else, please continue to read ☺.

Bob looks at how you take outside information into your mind and what happens for you to process it. The information from the outside world comes to you at a rate of 2-4Mbps. Stop and just think about that for a moment. Is it just me or is that totally mind-blowing? Between 2 and 4 MILLION bits of information per second!

If your logical thinking mind – your conscious mind – were to try and deal with that much information, you would blow your mind in a fraction of a second. It would be information overload.

Let me introduce you to your other mind. It's true, we have two minds and the second mind is the more powerful of the two. It can deal with 2-4Mbps AND the rest. It's the part of you that keeps your body running without you even thinking about it or knowing what it's doing. It keeps your heart beating, your lungs breathing, your digestive system digesting and your spleen… erm… spleening! One of its main roles is to keep you safe and it keeps your conscious mind safe too by making the 2-4Mbps smaller.

How does the brain process these thoughts?

The process is best described as a series of FILTERS that sort through the information.

The filters used are unique to you. They are based on your experiences, your memories, your values and standards, your attitudes, the way you make decisions, the culture you grew up in and how you process time, space, matter and energy. By reviewing all these elements that are unique to you, your unconscious mind makes the volume of information smaller by DELETING some of it, DISTORTING some of it and GENERALISING some of it to take out the details.

Once you have deleted, distorted and generalised through your filters, you give the information an INTERNAL REPRESENTATION or an inside re-presentation of the outside event through your filters. We can call this the MEANING that you give to the event. We'll look at this in a bit more detail in the coming chapters.

Once you have given it a meaning, you then know how you feel about it and what your emotional state is.

This emotional feeling dictates your physical response to the situation in terms of a reaction. These feelings and reactions form your behaviour so it's important to note that you may or may not get the result you want based on your behaviour, especially if you think back to those unmet needs we looked at in the last chapter. If you do not like the result in any area of your life or how you feel, then you have to go back and look at your behaviours, your emotions and the meanings that you assign to events.

A simple way to explain this is if you sat an English literature test, without reading the recommended text beforehand, the outcome would be far from ideal. How would you possibly be able to answer the questions? It wouldn't be any good blaming the person who had written the paper for the terrible result you got. You would have to look at what you needed to do differently, how you needed to act differently and how you wanted to feel differently. To learn and get a different result, you would have to assess what this test really meant to you.

When you really become aware of your inner thoughts, you can take care in choosing how you react so that the outcome is more beneficial.

Who can tell what thoughts I'm having?

Only you know your inner thoughts, but the way you react gives people an indication as to whether you are happy, sad, angry or indifferent.

Why do people react in different ways?

People react differently to the same event because of past experiences and future fears and desires. Remember that your filters are unique to you.

The way you think is a habit developed over time and because of past experiences. Your nervous system is wired to think this way, which is fine as long as your thoughts and reactions stay positive. If you tend to think negatively, or if you worry or get angry easily, you can change this thought pattern. You must *want* to change and it *will* take practice, but it is as simple as rewiring or rethinking your neural network (the nerves that run through your body passing on instructions about thoughts and actions). To put it simply, you are running old programmes that no longer serve you. It's like you're running on Windows 7 when you need to upgrade to Windows 10.

Technically, this is called 'neuroplasticity' (your brain's ability to reorganise itself by forming new neural networks) and it's the process by which you develop new thoughts.

Can you change how you react?

Yes, you can.

There are times in life when you won't achieve an outcome that you want or feel that you deserve. But let me tell you, if there's an aspect of your life that's not where you would like it to be, then it's down to one single reason – the story you tell yourself about why you can't have what you want.

If you can get in-tune with your internal dialogue, it becomes easy to stop and observe what you are saying.

Question your beliefs and the origins of your feelings and choose to change them for a better outcome. Ask yourself what the meaning you gave an event was that caused you to feel and act a certain way. Go back and ask, "Is the meaning I gave it really true? Could it have meant something else?"

If you change the meaning, you change the feeling, and this will consequently change how you act or react. We'll discuss this further in a later chapter.

Before we move on, make a quick note about a recent event that didn't have a favourable outcome and one that did.

- What were the main differences?

- How did you react to each?

- Who was involved?

- Where were you?

- What past experiences were relevant to these events?

Let's look in a little more detail and talk about your conscious and unconscious mind to fully appreciate how you can take control of your feelings and reactions.

"Follow your intuition, listening to your dreams, your inner voice to guide you."

Katori Hall

Chapter 10

What is your internal representation?

All of the stuff that goes on around you – the people you meet, the subjects you learn, the activities you get involved in, and the decisions you make about this stuff – comes from the 2-4Mbps of information you receive and 60,000 thoughts you have every day. Clearly you cannot be conscious of every single piece of information or thought, so how does it all work?

What is IR? Reality to virtual to reality again

I love that thought – we have our own virtual reality and it's true. You never experience an event directly. You experience it only through your filters and, as your filters are unique to you, you give it your own unique version of reality, which could be very different from other people's versions of that same event.

'Internal representation' (IR) or your 're-presentation' of the outside event, as mentioned in the previous chapter, is the name given to the process of your brain interpreting the external information it receives, assigning a meaning and an emotion, and creating a reaction.

It's pretty impressive. No, wait – YOU are freakin' impressive! Your unconscious mind deals with this information in a very sophisticated way, in a fraction of a second, in a way that you are not consciously aware of – WOW! How amazing is YOUR unconscious mind?!

Understanding the difference between your two minds

Let's recap from chapter 9 the concept of your two minds.

1. Your rational, CONSCIOUS MIND thinks logically and likes to understand and work things out. It also likes to think that it's in control when in fact…

2. Your UNCONSCIOUS MIND is the most powerful part of your entire being and is the one that's really in control.

Scientists say that you use only 10 per cent of your brain. That 10 per cent is used by your logical, conscious mind, but your unconscious mind, in my belief, handles the other 90 per cent.

Your unconscious mind is phenomenal. It is the first in line to deal with the 2-4Mbps of information you receive. Most of it, as you're realising, never reaches your conscious mind.

This part of you is so powerful that you don't have to stop and think about even taking in a breath. Remember that it keeps your lungs breathing, your digestive system digesting, your kidneys filtering and your spleen spleening! It never sleeps.

Rest and regenerate

Your conscious mind needs to switch off in order to rest and recuperate – it's perfectly logical. But while your conscious mind is recharging your 'awake' batteries, your unconscious mind is healing your entire body. It processes the day's information, embedding what you've learned and working stuff out so that when you wake up in the morning you feel fresh as a daisy.

Your unconscious mind has a job (among many others) to keep you safe. It's the one that triggers the fight-or-flight response introduced in chapter 3.

Managing the 2-4Mbps of information

As your unconscious mind is the first in line to deal with the 2-4Mbps bits of information, it dwindles them down to a more manageable 134bps of information. It still sounds like a massive amount of information to deal with, but this reduction enables you to add some level of context to an external situation. It's at this point that IR takes place, as the reduced information passes through a unique set of filters.

YOUR UNIQUE FILTERS GIVE MEANING TO A SITUATION

The same external situation can look very different in the eyes of two people once the information has been individually re-presented. That's because everyone has different filters.

Have you ever felt nervous in a situation where your friends felt comfortable? Maybe you really enjoyed watching a TV series, but you picked up vibes from another family member who appeared to dislike it in some way.

Individual filters cause people to interpret the exact same event, activity or news in a very different way. This is why some people don't like needles and others are indifferent. It's why some people like dogs and some prefer cats. It's why some people love a hot curry and others prefer a mild dish. It's why you might enjoy English literature, but your BFF loves maths. And so on.

What examples can you think of where you interpret something differently from your friends or family?

- What is the situation?

- How does it make you feel?

- What are the main differences?

- Can you think of a reason why your interpretation is different?

- What could happen to make you think otherwise about it?

Keep your answers at the front of your mind as we look at the three filters in more detail in the next chapters. But first…

Chapter 11

A little story with a big meaning

'If you are not the hero of your own story, then you're missing the whole point of your humanity.'

Steve Maraboli

There are three main reasons why you interpret and react to a situation differently from others. The filters that sort through the external information as it is processed in your mind will DELETE, DISTORT and GENERALISE it.

The previous few chapters were quite heavy going, so well done for sticking around ☺. Before we look at filters in more detail, I'd like to share a story with you that has always resonated with me. It's a powerful story and it will show you the extreme side of how external information is interpreted.

A story about destiny

Kick back, grab a drink or a snack and relax. It's not a long story, but I want you to think carefully about where it's leading and the underlying message you draw from it. This is a story that references God, but you don't have to support a particular religion, or even believe in God for that matter, to learn from it. What it will do is offer a deeper understanding about life and the choices you have.

Let's begin.

Right in the heart of America is an important town. It's important because it's slap bang in the middle of the continental landmass and it's a town of extremes. The climate is either hot or cold, windy or calm, or suffers from torrential rainfall or complete drought. It's tough living there.

The high mountains in the north collect water as rainfall or snow. This water consequently cascades downhill and forms a meandering river through the centre of the town.

Recently, the town suffered a major crisis because heavy rain had poured for a long period of time and the riverbanks burst close to the town's edge. Thankfully, the authorities organised an evacuation procedure and sent in coaches to transport the residents to safety. Most people left, but a few refused to leave, including one stubborn elderly gentleman. "I'm not leaving, this is my home," he shouted at the authorities. "I believe in God and he will save me." He had true faith, you might think.

The rain continued to pour for a few more days and the water level rose to cover the ground floor of the town's properties. The authorities were extremely worried about the remaining residents, so they sent in boats to evacuate those that had stayed. This time, everyone left apart from the elderly gentleman. He continued to shout, "This is my town and I shall not be leaving. I have faith in God, and he'll do the right thing for me." Reluctantly the authorities left after trying everything they could to encourage the man to leave.

A couple of days later there was no sign that the rain would cease. The water level continued to rise and eventually lapped at the house roofs. The elderly gentleman could be seen perched on top of his home, legs dangled either side of the roof. The authorities feared for his life, so they sent in a helicopter to save him. As a rescuer was lowered down on a rope from the helicopter to reach the elderly man, he could hear him shouting, "Leave me be; I am not going; God will save me." The man waved the helicopter away and once again the rescue mission was aborted.

Unfortunately, I'm sorry to say that the rain did not cease, and the elderly gentleman was swept away.

The story continues and the elderly gentleman's soul went to a place where souls go. He found himself in front of a pair of almighty gates and he was angry. He banged fiercely on the gates, demanding to be let in. Eventually, the gates creaked open and there stood St Peter who was in charge of all souls passing through the gates. He had a whole manner of qualifications, including a great understanding of human behaviour. Peter listened to the elderly man shouting and bawling, the anger and frustration so obviously consuming him. Peter calmly spoke to the gentleman. "Looking at it from your point of view, I can see where you are coming from…" But he was cut down immediately as the elderly man demanded to see God.

Reluctantly, Peter picked up the divine penthouse hotline to God. "Sorry to trouble you, sir, only I have a rather irate gentleman down here who says you've let him down and is adamant that he needs to see you – what would you like me to do?"

"Send him up," said God, and so the elderly gentleman was allowed to enter a celestial lift that ascended for what seemed like an eternity. When the doors finally opened, the elderly gentleman stood face-to-face with God. "You let me down big time; I had faith in you; I thought you would save me, and you let me down," he shouted in anger.

"What on earth do you mean I let you down?" God replied matter-of-factly. "Have you not learned how to use the gifts I gave you? Your five senses, your evolving brain and all the resources in the world? I sent coaches to evacuate you, followed by boats – I even organised a helicopter. In the next life, maybe you will learn to take more responsibility for your own actions, to make sensible choices and to accept help when offered." The elderly man was gobsmacked!

There you have it. So many signs, so many choices and so many different decisions made. What are you thinking now? What would you have done in this situation?

The story is by Julian Russell and has been adapted slightly from *The Magic of Metaphors*. You can take all kinds of meanings from this story, but it has a powerful message. There will be opportunities and chances in life that offer help and support. Ultimately you are in charge of the outcome of a situation and, believe it or not, you can change things in order to alter how you feel about a situation and your subsequent reaction or action.

Think about the choices you have

Think back to your childhood memories of bedtime storytelling.

- What was your favourite story?

- Why did you like it so much?

- Was it because the hero won in the end?

- Did the colourful illustrations in the book enchant you?

- Did you relate to one of the characters?

You build on existing stories by expanding the adventures they carry. You create your own life story every single day, so let me ask you a question: how's it evolving so far? What's the immediate answer that came to mind? Jot it down.

If you are less than happy with your answer, think about where you lie on a scale of 1 to 10, with 10 feeling magnificent. If there's room for improvement, it may be because you are seeing things from a negative point of view or you are giving control of your life to others – just like the elderly gentleman in the story. Remember, the only reason you don't have the life you want is the story you tell yourself about why you can't have it.

Hold that thought and let's move on to stretch and challenge your thinking once more. Let's help you to grow and become magnificent.

"Confidence is knowing who you are and not changing it a bit because someone's version of reality is not your reality."

Shannon L Alder

Chapter 12
Filters – making sense of sensory input

"Your perception may not be my reality."

Aporva Kala

Around 2-4m bits of information every second and 60,000 thoughts each day is a lot. Wow!

The powerful and continual filtering process in your mind reduces the volume of external information you receive as sensory input — through your eyes, ears, nose, mouth, even touch — by DELETING, DISTORTING and GENERALISING. This is known as the Communication Model in neurolinguistic programming (NLP) — a field of study about thoughts and behaviours.

Determine the present through the past and future

Your mind's filters trawl through memories, past experiences and decisions. They weigh up your beliefs, values and attitudes, the culture you grew up in and the education you've absorbed to date. It happens in a split second and gives you a meaning to a situation. You're amazing!

It's like social scrolling

Picture yourself scrolling through your Facebook, Instagram, YouTube or Snapchat feed. No, this isn't an excuse to leave this book and grab your phone: just imagine your index finger running its own marathon on the screen as you see tiny glimpses of comments, photos or videos.

What encourages you to read a post, watch a video or click on a link to find out more? It takes seconds, but somehow your mind picks up on a trigger. Maybe it's a colour, a word or a visual that appears familiar or ignites curiosity. Can you think of the last post that stopped your scrolling finger? What was it? It's a very similar process that takes place in your unconscious mind as it filters through sensory input, only way, way faster and you're not aware that it's happening.

Where has your big toe disappeared to?

When did you last feel your big toe? It's still there (I hope). It's always been there, but it's only when you draw attention to it, or any part of your body for that matter, with your conscious mind that you realise it's there and you feel its presence. So, why do you forget about it? Well, you don't forget as such; it's more that your unconscious mind has chosen to delete the feelings of your big toe from your conscious mind because there are more important things to focus on – like watching a quirky YouTube video, for example ☺.

Deletion – it's not relevant

Mental deletion is an automatic process that tunes out parts of your experience because you regard them as irrelevant. It may be that something took place, but the impact was so insignificant that you simply forgot that it ever happened. It may also be that you know something so well that it becomes a habit and you don't consciously think about the actions required to do it. A bit like brushing your teeth or the action of sipping a drink.

As an event takes place, you focus on the parts that appear most important at that time and the rest is deleted from your conscious mind.

Distortion – it might not be true

When information is distorted, you misrepresent a situation. It can happen one of two ways: either you blow up a situation way bigger than it is, or you make things seem far more insignificant than they are.

Situations become a big deal when you overthink them. The meaning of a current situation might draw from a past experience that didn't go so well. Or you might worry about a future outcome because it's uncertain, as you've never experienced it before. When this happens, you are tempted to fill in the gaps with information that may be wrong, thereby distorting the reality of what is going to take place.

Young people often distort information because of a lack of self-belief or confidence in their own abilities. If you are given a compliment, for example, you may shrug it off because your internal dialogue and self-doubt doesn't believe it to be true.

Situations can also be distorted if you, or the others around you, use the wrong language to explain it. If someone says a pizza is really spicy, you may think that you won't enjoy it, but when you take a bite it's delicious and not spicy at all.

Generalisation – making assumptions

When you generalise information, you make a judgment to simplify a situation or experience. Take that spicy pizza. If you taste pizza for the first time and it's super spicy, too hot for your taste buds to enjoy the experience, you may generalise that all pizzas are hot and spicy. You may decide never to eat pizza again, but it's not the pizza that is spicy, it's just the topping – and pizzas have a great many toppings to choose from.

How many times have you said, "Everybody always says that?" or "Everybody always does that?"

- Why is that?

- Who is everybody?

- How many are there?

- Can you name everybody?

- When exactly did they say or do that?

- And what is THAT?

- What did they say or do?

When you put the detail back into a situation, you consider the information on an individual level. Doing it this way does take longer and that's why the finer details are often stripped out. You just don't have the time to process everything on a conscious level.

It's all about perception.

Why do you do the things you do?

Think about a situation that made you angry. It could be something you were involved in, witnessed from a distance or just heard about after it had taken place. Describe the event in general terms and consider the following:

- Where were you?

- Who was involved?

- How did you perceive this event?

- How did you react?

- How did it make you feel?

- What words did you express at the time?

- What consequences did your reaction have on you?

- What consequences did your reaction have on those around you?

- What information did you delete that might have made you feel differently if you hadn't?

- What information did you potentially distort?

- What information did you generalise, and was it right or wrong to do so?

The more detail you can use to describe this situation the better, because it will help you to reflect on what really took place. Why do you think this situation happened? Would you use different words to describe it now? Would you act differently if it happened again?

Try the same exercise, but this time think about a positive situation. Compare your answers. What is different? I guarantee you'll get an eye-opening moment!

"It takes courage to grow up and become who you really are."

e.e cummings

Chapter 13

State – choose your words with care

"All we have to decide is what to do with the time that is given to us."

J R R Tolkien

Your words create your reality

Your emotional state is reflected in the words you use to describe a situation, which also define your behaviours and how you react. If you choose to use emotionally charged words, positively or negatively, you will feel emotionally charged, positively or negatively. Your words create your reality.

You are responsible for the words you speak

Once you give a meaning to an external situation, you have a choice about how to react. Slowing down to take a few seconds, even minutes, to think through how you respond can make a huge difference.

The classroom kneejerk

Can you remember a classroom incident taking place that caused mixed reactions? Perhaps a few of your fellow students were mucking around and giggling. It was probably an innocent situation, but the giggling might have outraged your teacher and things got out of hand. Maybe a controversial topic was presented, and a student fiercely disagreed with the material. What reaction did you have? Did you relate to your teacher or to a fellow student?

You already know that people react differently to the same incident because of the unconscious mind's filtering process. The emotional state that follows can be positive or negative and will determine your use of language, tone of voice, facial expression and general body language.

If you are outraged your voice might be high-pitched, your choice of words strong and your face angry. If you are upset your voice might be quiet, your words limited and your face anxious.

Choose your words wisely

Think again about the classroom incident. Was it mildly irritating and got on your nerves a bit or was it *so annoying* that you felt hot, irritated and couldn't think clearly? Be careful how you describe it. Why do you think certain words come to mind?

If you think carefully before you react and choose neutral or positive words, you won't feel angry, upset or unclear. You will feel differently about the situation, calmer and in control. Boom! That's RESILIENT THINKING kicking in.

Free yourself from past negatives

You can't change your past because you can't yet travel back in time. Your past provides life's important experiences and lessons so you can learn from them, not get stuck in them. But the past does shape the way you are today.

If you train your brain to give new and improved meanings to external situations, you can go from being disempowered to being totally empowered and in control of your life. The only thing you have control over is inside your mind – Bob shows you this.

You have no control over external events, but you can choose how you react to them. Take responsibility for yourself and never put your feelings and behaviours in the hands of others.

Change the story you tell yourself

A lot of how you feel, the activities you take part in and the things you do originate from the stories you tell yourself and the thoughts you have between your two ears. Let me explain by describing a recent conversation I found myself listening to.

Conversations that paint a picture

During one of my working-from-home days, I popped into the local coffee shop for some lunch and a break from the computer. Sipping a black coffee and eyeing up the sweet treats, I was mentally drawn into the conversation a bunch of ladies sitting at the next table were having. Have you ever done that? You've been minding your own business then all of a sudden, a few words capture your attention, your ears twitch and you're hooked. You feel a bit like an impostor, but you can't help but listen.

The ladies were chatting about holidays, where they had been and where they would love to visit. I mentally added a few to my own travel list.

As the conversation progressed, more exotic places were suggested until one lady commented that "it would be impossible to visit there because you'd need to take at least one to two months to make it worthwhile" and "it would be so expensive". The comment got me thinking, "Why is it impossible? Why would you need so much time? And why should it be so expensive?"

Switch the story around to what does work

Last year I flew 6,000 miles to the west coast of America to attend a two-day event. It took longer to get there and back than the time I spent at the event and people look at me as though I'm crazy when I explain this. You know what? It was beyond worth it and I certainly wasn't going to let the *limits of my beliefs or the beliefs of others* stop me from doing something that I knew would be enriching for me.

Think about this from a completely different viewpoint: I got to spend time with some of my closest colleagues and friends from around the world. I was able to catch up with people I'd not seen for ages and hear about their adventures. I was fortunate to hang out with top neuroscience strategists (the really clever people who understand what makes our nervous systems and brains tick) and learn from them to expand my knowledge. And to top it, I got to stay in an awesome floating house on a river.

I created many memories of friendships, mentorships and new experiences and the trip made a huge difference to my life. It was a win-win situation.

Stretch your imagination

Now I've shared this with you, are you ready to stretch and challenge your thinking? I wanted to challenge the ladies in the coffee shop, but I needed to mind my own business.

Imagine a place that you always wanted to visit. Think of somewhere that you've attached negatives to, such as you can't get there, you don't have enough time or enough money, you're too young, you don't have anyone to go with, you wouldn't know what to do when you get there, or that it would be too hard to organise. Make a note of the destination and your reasons for the adventure not becoming reality.

Question the negative reasons:

- Why can't you get there?

- Why do you think you can't afford it?

- Why do you have to go with someone?

- Why are you too young?

Now look at the options. If you think you can't afford a trip, is there a volunteer or charity venture you can enrol on? Is there a way for you to exchange your skills? What can you plan during your school holidays, or where can you seek to meet a new set of friends to work together for a common goal?

The only thing holding you back from doing some of the things you want to do is you and the stories you tell yourself.

Once you start to notice the negative thoughts that block progress or achievement, you'll see that they are always the same. *Work on alternative ways of thinking.*

Create your own positive and aspirational story

Anything is possible once you *remove self-imposed limitations.* Make a list of what you really want to do and seek ways to make them doable – it's just a matter of time and approach.

You are never too old, too young or too nervous and anything is within reach if you believe it to be. If you really want it, you will always get there, always be able to commit and find time. What if you are just the right age, the time is perfect and it's available somewhere at a fraction of the cost?

Be bold, be strong, be curious and be resilient.

"The world is big and I want to have a good look at it before it gets dark."

John Muir

Chapter 14

The four pillars of resilience – build your fortress

"Life is full of surprises. Not all these surprises are pleasant, so you need to be ready for what life brings you."

Unknown

You may have realised at some point during your reading of this book that you (sometimes) haven't been handling things as well as you could have done. You still might think that some situations (or even people) are hard to deal with.

That's OK. *You can change that.* And the next six chapters will show you how by using a little (actually, rather big and formidable) technique called RESILIENCE.

Grab a (healthy) bite to eat, rehydrate or nip to the loo before you begin.

Resilience will help you to tackle anything

Keep Bob with you through the few next chapters and use him as a summary of the previous chapters.

You experience life through learning, being curious, approaching challenges, and setting goals. For you as a young person, it can be tough to handle challenging situations because you face many for the first time. You haven't yet built up a bank of past experiences to guide you through to the decisions you make, which then help you become more resilient. You need obstacles to challenge you in order to learn valuable lessons, to build your skills, and to be able to share ideas and experiences with others. Put simply, *resilience is your superpower of bouncebackability.*

Who stole my easy life?

One minute you're pottering along in life; everything is good; you have no stresses then – *bam* – life *does* happen. And it can be immense when you're a teenager. Something occurs, that often comes from nowhere, and it just rocks your entire world. It doesn't have to be something catastrophic, although a death, illness or separation in the family can be the cause of severe distress. It could just be a series of little things that mount up and suddenly the reality of what they all mean hits you. And you're not sure which way to turn. *Resilience will guide you.*

Life happens, so what is resilience and how can it help me get through hard times?

When you think about the word 'resilience' what does it mean to you?

You might think about setbacks you have experienced and how hard it's been to recover from something that happened in the past. Maybe your parents separated, you suffered a humiliating experience at school, or were unsuccessful somehow at something you desperately wanted to achieve.

If you're unsure, the American Psychological Association's summary of the key factors of resilience may be helpful: www.apa.org/topics/resilience

- Build connections
    - Prioritise relationships
    - Join a group

- Foster wellness
    - Take care of your body
    - Practise mindfulness
    - Avoid negative outlets

- Find purpose
    - Help others
    - Be proactive
    - Move towards your goals
    - Look for opportunities for self-discovery

- Embrace healthy thoughts
    - Keep things in perspective
    - Accept change
    - Maintain a hopeful outlook
    - Learn from your past

- Seek help

Resilience doesn't mean the absence of stress or difficult situations. Being flexible instead of rigid demonstrates resilience. It's the notion of pick yourself back up, dust yourself off and away you go again. Some people are better at being resilient than others, but it is most definitely a skill that can be learned if you think about it as four pillars:

- Resilient thinking
- Effective relationships
- Managing emotions
- Building strengths

Stand up to your challenges

The only way to build your resilience is to face up to challenging and unexpected situations. You will always have them, and overcoming them will shape who you are.

People stand strong when they are resilient because they survived a tough challenge. This might conjure up an image in your mind of someone you know – a friend, parent, teacher or role model. People weren't made this way. They were tested and challenged and, as a result, have become stronger through dealing with harsh situations in a positive way.

The biggest hurdle against resilience

The single biggest factor obstructing your resilience is your inner voice. Remember the 60,000 daily thoughts and the unhelpful ones that just go round and round like a video loop in your mind?

Thoughts will eventually become things in your reality, so if you think negative thoughts you will start to develop those negative behaviours that we looked at in chapter 8.

What does a slammed door say to you?

If you were with me now and I got up to leave the room and slammed the door behind me, what would you think?

- I was angry

- I was upset

- I was angry because of something you had said or done

Let's flip those thoughts for a second and think about what else the slamming door could mean. Perhaps a window was open in the next room and the breeze caught the door as I went to close it, so the additional force made it bang? Could it be that the door was a fire door and normally it would close slowly on its own, but for some reason the safety mechanism was broken so it slammed shut quickly?

Can you see how these *alternative meanings are still possible*, and that they are not negative in any way?

In order to become resilient, you need to think in a resilient way. Remember IR and the difference between your conscious and unconscious mind? Well that's where your resilient thinking starts.

"The best things in life are unexpected because there were no expectations."

Eli Khamorov

Chapter 15
How to build resilient thinking

"Just sitting here on the corner of awesome and bombdiggity."

Unknown

Resilient thinking – strengthen your mind

It sounds like a solution to all your problems – right? Well not quite, but it will put you in the best place to deal with unhelpful stuff. You'll be a better person and **you'll rock any situation if you train your brain** always to think positively. You'll find solutions easier and quicker too.

Ten-day 'mind your mind neuro challenge'

You're going to love this!

The whole purpose of the challenge is not to dwell on negative thoughts or emotions for 10 consecutive days. Naturally, you may still have negative thoughts, but the objective is to never focus on them for more than two minutes.

The trick is to *catch negative thinking and consciously change your thoughts* and emotions within a two-minute timeframe. High five if you're able to do this after a few days, but here's the stinger: if the negative thoughts remain after two minutes or if they come back later the same day, you have to reset the 10 days. Yep! Sorry! You have to go back to day one!

Here's the motivational bit: the reset will absolutely happen. I've not met anyone who hasn't had to start over at least a couple of times. After a bad phone call with a friend, reading an uncomfortable social media post or being frustrated with a piece of homework, it'll happen. AND you are still building resilient thinking by the sheer act of resetting the 10 days because **you are aware** of it. See, you're already becoming more magnificent.

Be patient

I know that 'patience' is cancelled from your vocabulary between the ages of 10 and about 22, but please take your time. Persistence is a wonderful skill, especially at your age.

When I was first introduced to this concept, it took me four weeks to achieve 10 consecutive days. But once I had gone through the exercise and achieved a successful outcome – WOW! I've never looked back. And neither will you. What you're doing is going through the process of reprogramming your neural network to think positively all the time.

Here's the motivational bit (for real this time!) There'll be no going back. Your *life will be more enjoyable* and situations you once found stressful that bothered you for ages will become a breeze. How cool is that?

Still need a little help to think positively?

If this seems like a mammoth task and you feel a little unsure about where to start, fear not, here are 20 tips that will totally help you make this work.

You don't have to do all 20. The tips are designed to positively support you to 'mind your mind' and change your emotions for the better. I promise it'll be a game changer. Choose tips that work for you.

Twenty tips to eradicate your negative thoughts

1. I'll come back to this at the end...

2. Find your power move.

   It's a quick move with power and enables you to reset your thoughts.

   Find something that works for you – a punch in the air, the clap of your hands or a fist bump to your chest.

3. Ask power questions.

   What are you grateful for? What could you be grateful for? Who do you love? Who loves you? What are you proud of? What are you excited about in your life?

   Come up with a series of questions that you can answer honestly.

4. Question the negative thought.

   Find at least six different meanings for why the negative thought happened.

   Ask what else it could mean and ensure that some of the reasons are positive.

   Focus only on the positives in the future.

5. Invest in a stretchy man.

   Or a stretchy animal or food or whatever (have you never seen stretchy sausages or eggs?) – get a stress ball or a foamy squidgy shape to keep in your bag.

   If you think about something negative, find the stretchy entity and give it a squeeze – it's guaranteed to make you smile.

6. Jump up and shout, "Woohoo!" Homer Simpson style.

   It might sound odd, but I promise it will change your state of mind for the better and it doesn't matter if people look at you in amazement – never worry about what other people think.

7. Find pictures of amazing memories on your phone and revisit the joy of the moment.

   This is happiness literally in the palm of your hand.

8. Play a power anthem.

   Sing out loud, play the air guitar and get moving.

   The focus and flow will make you feel 10 times better.

9. Do a dance movement guaranteed to give you a little oomph.

10. Do a twirl.

11. Skip up and down the living room, down the garden path or out of the classroom door (when it's time to, of course).

12. Splash in a puddle.

13. Play like an aeroplane.

    Pretend you're a kid again, open your arms and make the 'weee' flying sound – it's revitalisation in seconds.

14. Buy stickers.

    Invest in smiley faces, stars and hearts, comments that state "You are awesome", "You're a true superstar".

    Put one on yourself and give them out to people around you – who doesn't love a sticker?

15. Carry out random acts of kindness.

    Cheer someone up by waving, smiling or giving a kind comment – this will instantly change your focus.

16. Keep a jar of inspirational quotes.

    Make your own quotes from magazine cut-outs, create a Pinterest board or buy a card pack.

    These quotes will be your personal fortune cookies or uplifting angel cards.

17. Give someone a hug.

    Hugs are fantastic: they release endorphins, which are your own internal feel-good factors.

18. Ask Siri, Alexa or your chosen voice assistant to tell you a joke – it's hilarious what they come out with.

19. Give someone a sincere compliment.

    Do this in person, send a message or write it down on a Post-it note – be true.

20. Sip a cup of tea and savour a piece of cake.

    This great British tradition always makes everything appear better.

Start today and think positively every step of the way.

Wait a minute...

I bet you thought I'd forgotten – let's look at the number one tip for eradicating your negative thoughts. I wanted to come back to this one because it's probably the most powerful.

Memorise your favourite incantation

Let me explain what I mean by 'incantation'.

You may have heard of affirmations and mantras, which are similar to incantations with a subtle difference. An affirmation is a phrase that you say over and over again and a mantra is an expression you say when meditating or relaxing deeply. Both are used to help to calm your mind.

I like to think that an incantation has a deeper purpose. Saying an incantation puts a spell on you. It's a kind of self-hypnosis that uses all or most of your senses to become much more powerful. I'll share a few with you in chapter 18 because they are excellent for building your strengths.

"This is the year I will be stronger, braver, kinder and unstoppable. This year I will be fierce."

Unknown

Chapter 16

How to build effective relationships

*"Don't change so people will like you.
Be yourself and the right people will
love the real you."*

Unknown

Effective relationships are connections with people who are supportive, positive and encouraging. *Eliminate everyone from your life who does not meet these criteria.*

Relationship resilience for inner peace

Let me share a well-known literary piece to illustrate relationship resilience. It resonates so strongly with me that I carry it with me every day as symbols tattooed on my wrist.

> People come into your life for a reason, a season, or a lifetime.
>
> When you figure out which one it is, you will know what to do for each person.
>
> When someone is in your life for a reason, it is usually to meet a need you have expressed.
>
> They have come to assist you through a difficulty, to provide you with guidance and support, to aid you physically, emotionally or spiritually.
>
> They may seem like a godsend and they are.
>
> They are there for the reason you need them to be.

Then without any wrongdoing on your part or at an inconvenient time, this person will say something or do something to bring the relationship to an end, sometimes they die, sometimes they walk away, sometimes they act up and force you to take a stand.

What you must realise is this, that our need has been met, our desire fulfilled, their work is done, the prayer you sent up has been answered and now it is time to move on.

Some people come into your life for a season because your turn has come to share, grow or learn. They bring you an experience of peace or make you laugh.

They may teach you something you've never done; they usually give you an unbelievable amount of joy.

Believe it; it is real. But only for a season.

Lifetime relationships teach you lifetime lessons − things you must build upon in order to have a solid emotional foundation.

Your job is to accept the lesson, love the person and put into practice what you have learned to use in all your other relationships and areas of your life.

It is said that love is blind, but friendship is clairvoyant.

Friends, family members, teachers, work colleagues and strangers come into your life for a purpose. Not all relationships seem positive at the time, but they serve a purpose.

Relationships for a reason

A reason may be a response to a request for help or information or to solve a problem. Perhaps you were feeling down and a stranger in a supermarket queue smiled at you in a way that it lifted your mood. The moment was brief, but the outcome was just what you needed at the time.

Your path will cross with someone else's for a minute, an hour, a few hours, or a few days. When your need is met that person is gone, their job complete.

Relationships for a season

Often, a lesson learned, a question answered, or a gift given or received takes longer to complete. The need is bigger, therefore a season (not a change in weather) is required. Your paths will cross for several months or years, but once the need is met, you move on.

Relationships for a lifetime

Sometimes you will gain the gift of a lifetime in a relationship or career choice – perhaps with a family member, a close friend or someone sharing a journey with you through a career or as a loving partner.

Getting to grips with relationship resilience

Sometimes relationships go wrong and at times you will feel:

- Pain

- Disappointment

- Uncertainty

- Anger

- Sadness

- Guilt

- Vulnerability

This is OK – it means you're human and it's the paradox of the two essential needs: connection (love) and significance. Remember? Resilience gives you the ability to handle hurt more easily, to overcome feelings of being let down, to forgive and to accept what has happened and move on.

Surround yourself with effective relationships

You will become like the people you spend most of your time with. This is fact. To be resilient, surround yourself with people who support, inspire and challenge you to be a better person. Choose to be with those who listen and empathise, but don't allow you to wallow in self-pity or worry for any length of time.

The things you value about friends, family members, teachers, managers or work colleagues will differ. They might make you laugh, feel happy, loved, safe or healthy.

Time is precious and limited so cherish every single minute.

The people you spend time with and the activities you participate in need to be enjoyable. What's the point in doing something you don't enjoy? It's a waste of your time, right? Of course, you may still be in education and have other compulsory commitments that are less than enjoyable for you but see them as part of your journey for greater things in life.

Who is in your life right now?

First, take a moment to think about the people in your life. Whoever they are and wherever they are, write down their names. It might help you to identify them better if you use subheadings to indicate how you know them, such as school, family, friends, after-school swimming class, music class etc. There will be lots of people so take your time – this exercise is not meant to be a quick win.

Who do you like?

When you are finished, review the names on your list and highlight those that you enjoy spending time with.

Separately, make a note of how they make you feel and why you enjoy spending time with them.

- What benefits do they bring to your relationship?

- Are they thoughtful, trustworthy, adventurous or inspiring?

- Where do they appear in your life?

- How do you spend time with them?

It could be your supportive, hilarious best friend. It might be a parent who never judges and gives you unconditional love. Or it could be an encouraging teacher, mentor or coach who believes in your ability and pushes you to achieve better results. Jot down how you feel about these people and their qualities.

Who are you indifferent to?

Second, carry out the same exercise, highlighting the people who are in your life, for whatever reason, but don't add any real value. You wouldn't go out of your way to spend time with them and they are present in your life only because they share a class or workplace with you, for example.

Who don't you like?

Finally, use a different colour or shape to highlight a third list of people. You don't like spending time with these people and given the choice you would rule them out of your life. Jot down why this is. They might be:

- A school bully

- Lazy

- A gossip

- Untrustworthy

- Negative and always moaning

How do they make you feel and what behaviours do they display? Do they laugh at you or humiliate you? Perhaps they steal or take illegal substances and try to pressure you or others into doing the same.

Once you have completed your three lists – take a break if you need to – review your first and third list and become aware of the differences. What do you notice?

Your first step to building effective relationships is to understand *what makes good and bad relationships*. Now you have proof of what each looks like, you can concentrate on what you feel is a useful and rewarding relationship to have.

Practise being the person you would want to spend more time with.

"Appreciate good people.
They are hard to come by."

Unknown

Chapter 17

How to build resilience in order to manage your emotions

"When it rains look for rainbows. When it's dark look for stars."

Unknown

The kid who feels no emotional upset when bad stuff happens is not resilient. The kid who fails miserably, feels like crap, wants to scream and shout, and run and hide, but survives to play another day without being resentful or blaming the world is resilient.

Is this you? Do you know anyone like this?

Displaying emotions can attract a 'snowflake' label, which isn't pretty and glistening. Being labelled this way adds to the pressures of being a teenager because it implies that you melt at the slightest thing, be it a new task, an uncertain situation or a confrontation. It suggests weakness and nervousness, and for the person being labelled, it can result in a lack of confidence, self-doubt and even self-loathing.

Riding the emotional ups and downs

While these emotions are quite normal (for anyone), you need techniques to *stay strong and positive*. Meltdowns, breakdowns, high anxiety, depression and even suicidal thoughts come from a belief that everything happening to you is out of your control. If you think that it's not your fault, that you have no power to make it stop, or that other people make your life miserable, this weakens your inner resilience. If you encounter bullies and negative people, it can be difficult to ignore their comments when your resilience is low.

The most powerful antidote is realising that these thoughts and comments are not true. They're a bunch of lies and with the right mindset you can discover how to *have life happen for you and not to you.*

You will not be the only person who fails a test, says the wrong thing, misses an important event, has an accident or breaks something. These things also offer the opportunity to meet one or more of your six human needs; using a poor behaviour at an 8, 9 or 10 out of 10, you can then get stuck using that behaviour. Why not instead use it as an opportunity to learn and grow, move on and become more resilient than ever?

It happens. You can't change it. Accept it. Move on. Build emotional resilience to allow you to do this. Take back control in your life, in your thoughts and in the way that you feel. Think of all the cool stuff you will achieve.

Do you turn into a monster when it gets cold and wintery?

Does the lack of daylight and onset of gloomy weather turn you into a sad soul? Do you know someone who gets down in the dumps during the winter? It's actually a thing, you know. Seasonal affective disorder (SAD) affects as many as one in three people in the UK and more females than males. It really shouldn't be referred to as SAD because that's a negative emotion!

It's difficult to understand how to cope with SAD when you're a teen because some of it may be down to age and changing hormones. But it does often start in your teenage years so now is the ideal time to look closely at how you feel.

Symptoms to watch out for include:

- Mood swings

- Low energy levels

- Sociable anxieties

- Feeling irritable

- Sleeping more

- Finding it hard to wake up

- Eating more, especially craving carbs (bread, potatoes and sweet treats)

- Lacking interest in things you normally enjoy

Remember, SAD is not an excuse for you to hibernate or a reason to ignore opportunities to get out and about. This is about recognition, taking responsibility and modifying your behaviour to adapt to the season and stay emotionally positive. I mentioned SAD because many people are aware of it, but the condition is also like a metaphor for when you feel in a dark place, lost and unmotivated.

It helps to eat healthily and stay hydrated. Eating junk food is not an excuse because you feel tired and don't want to prepare anything. Consuming more energy drinks is not an excuse because you have no energy. We'll look at this in more detail towards the end of the book.

Crying is good for you!

When was the last time you had a good cry?

- Did someone cause you to cry?
- Was it because of a painful accident?
- Was it because of an overwhelming situation?
- Was it at a happy event such as a wedding?

Some people say that crying is for wimps and you shouldn't cry in public. I suppose it's safe to say that you need to choose your company if you have a heavy tearful episode where your nose runs, and you can't breathe in between your sobs. But *it is scientifically proven that crying is good for you.*

The science behind your tears

The mechanism for crying is inbuilt. It wasn't an evolutionary accident and it is not a disorder, weakness or an action to apologise for.

In the 1970s, a University of Minnesota tear expert (what a cool job), Dr William Frey, analysed the chemical make-up of tears resulting from several experiments: chopping an onion, irritation from a piece of dirt, watching a sad movie and so on. (Can you relate to sobbing at a heroic animal film or a tragic love story? I sure can!)

Anyway, there are two main types of tears:

- Reflexive tears protect your eyes by flushing out foreign bodies and keeping them moist and lubricated

- Emotional tears occur from a heightened emotional state

Interestingly, this and subsequent experiments suggest that the main function of emotional tears is to help your body to reduce its stress levels by purging excess hormones and proteins. You could liken it to opening a window to let out a bad smell or hot stuffy air, balancing the atmosphere with fresh air so that you don't feel sick or to avoid overheating. Crying uses a similar response, but for a different purpose – to balance your emotions by calming your mood. *Crying is your built-in valve to release excess pressure and help you to manage your emotions.*

Still think crying is for babies?

If you have a tough shell and this all seems a bit childish, think again. Read the facts below and consider how having a good cry can be a positive reaction. Maybe you've experienced something similar.

1. **Stress reducer**

   When you feel anxious or worried, you produce a chemical known as adrenocorticotrophic hormone or 'ACTH' for short (because I can't pronounce it!). If you produce a large amount of ACTH it stimulates the release of the stress hormone cortisol, which instructs changes in your body to help reduce stress levels. Both chemicals are present in emotional tears, which suggests *a good sob removes stress.* And if you're honest, you do feel calmer and more resilient after a good cry.

2. Mood improver

Emotional tears contain endorphins, which are your body's natural feel-good factors. They provide pain relief and improve your mood. Get as many as you can!

3. Antibacterial agent

Lysozyme is a naturally occurring enzyme found in emotional tears, and can destroy up to 95% of bacteria in your eyes within 10 minutes. How cool is that? When your eyes start to water, they wash out foreign bodies and kill anything that shouldn't be there.

4. Calming agent

Emotional tears genuinely lower your blood pressure, resulting in a steadier pulse and calmer behaviour.

5. Positively proactive

Crying gives you a sense of letting it all out. You can move on instead of holding things within, holding on or holding back. Suppressed emotions can build up and even if you think you're keeping a tight lid on things, negative feelings seep out in physical ailments such as acne, muscle tension and poor sleeping patterns. Holding on to negative emotions can cause dis-ease or disease. Many serious illnesses have their root cause in unresolved suppressed emotions.

6. **External comforter**

Imagine this. When you see someone crying, your instinct is to offer comfort, right? To give a big hug or offer a few words of support.

Need a bear hug?

Hugging is an excellent mood enhancer and has been proven to reduce the amount of cortisol (that hormone again) in your body to aid stress reduction. Hugging releases oxytocin, another feel-good hormone that lowers blood pressure and creates a feeling of belonging. And here's an added bonus: if you hug for longer, you also get a boost in serotonin, which is your happy hormone. This will definitely put you in a good mood. Woohoo – who said you couldn't control your emotions?

"Know that whoever is trying to bring you down is already below you."

Boonaa Mohammed

Chapter 18

Power up and build your strengths

"Good habits formed at youth make all the difference."

Aristotle

Fancy a fresh start?

It's great to be at the point of a fresh start. To have a new beginning, something exciting to look forward to and be able to make dreams come true. When was the last time you felt the anticipation of something new? I love a fresh start; they come in many shapes and forms such as a new year resolution, the start of a new school year, a new subject, getting fit, learning a new sport or hobby, or even starting a job.

A new beginning is a time to give up bad habits and seek different, positive behaviours that allow you to be the best you can be. Creating a vision board or setting goals will help you to focus on what you really want to achieve. It will keep you on track and act as a reminder to stride forward and reach out for what you desire.

And the best thing is that you can decide in any moment of any day to make NOW a fresh start!

Make your future how you want it to be

Use this simple template to create a set of goals and start thinking innovatively about what's important – start a fresh page or sheet ☺.

Create your goals around the following titles:

- **Super Six:** six goals focused around your education, your career, your future professional self

- **Fantastic Four:** four personal goals centred around your social life, emotional, physical and mental wellbeing

Split the goals so that you have more geared towards your future career because it is one of the main driving factors in being able to achieve your personal goals. You need money, right?

Think about the two sets of goals as ones that you want to achieve over the next 12 months and make them your prime focus. Make sure they are realistic and achievable. A dream job or ideal uni placement may still be a couple of years down the line, so be careful not to set yourself up for failure. Having said that, do throw in some fun, a bit crazy and a bit (in the eyes of other people who don't know how amazing you are) unrealistic goals too ☺.

Other things will come along, and you may need to reprioritise, but you have to start somewhere. Take some time to 'chunk the goals down' so that you have a quarterly, monthly, weekly, even a daily focus that will take you one step further to achieving each goal. It's OK to shuffle things around a bit: obstacles will happen.

Examples could include achieving top grades in your exams, starting an after-school course, reconnecting with a friend, securing your first Saturday job, attending a further education open day or visiting an attraction you've never been to before.

Celebrate your achievements

This you must absolutely do when you hit a goal. Looking back over what you've achieved can provide inspiration if you're struggling for goal motivation.

The process of *taking time to reflect and appreciate what you've achieved is extremely fulfilling.* It's another chance to reward yourself and take pride in how you came to this point.

Look back at the photos on camera roll, check your social profiles, review your calendar or journal, even pull out the photo albums (if you still have any) and think about the following:

- What did you do last year?
- Who did you participate with?

- How did you celebrate what you achieved?

- Which places did you go to?

- What experiences did you encounter?

- Which new people did you meet?

- How did the above make you feel at the time?

- How do you feel now, reflecting?

I guarantee this exercise will make you smile and reinvigorate forgotten adventures. Relive the enjoyment and laughter, and cherish these proud moments. Remembering good times will build strength of character and remind you of what makes you happy. You'll remain more positive and seek more of what you enjoy – learning moments, romantic moments, insightful moments, future-changing moments or fist bump moments. Now what were those 10 goals again?

Share your thoughts with us on social media:

- www.instagram.com/ignition.rocks

- www.facebook.com/IgnitionYP

- www.twitter.com/ignition2017

Use it or lose it!

Imagine sitting at home all day watching the TV. I'm not talking about news bulletins, David Attenborough nature programmes or cultural documentaries. I'm referring to soaps or cartoons or bingeing on box sets.

- What new information are you learning about the world?

- What outdoor adventures are stimulating your mind?

- How are you interacting with the people around you?

The act of learning and being curious is enriching and builds strength from within. It gives you a thirst to seek more about what you love. But you need to get out and away from inactive habits. Stop living life vicariously through others in reality TV shows and YouTube and get into the real world to live YOUR life and have your own REAL experiences.

Newfound knowledge will increase your mind's capacity by proactively creating new neural networks – groups of nerve cells within your body. By seeking to solve problems and choosing to question what's around you, every time you think a thought, belief or value you make it stronger and as your neural network gets bigger it becomes less of an effort. You'll be a champion at whatever you want in no time – well, with a bit of work and effort.

If you want to be happy every day, stimulate a neural network that allows you to feel cheerful and participate in fun activities. You can change your identity, your perception of situations and your beliefs.

It doesn't take 21 days to form a new habit; you just need to repeat what you want to do and feel. Use your 10 goals to stay on course.

The magical science that helps you to stay resilient

Here's the amazing thing: you already have the foundations of resilience built into your brain. You have what is known as a *reticular activating system* or RAS for short. The system notices the things that mean more to you and makes you aware of them more frequently by filtering out the unnecessary details and *focusing on what is important to you* – remember how powerful this process is?

If you *concentrate on positive relationships, positive emotions and positive actions,* your thoughts and behaviours will automatically become more prominent because your brain is prioritising them. How cool is that?

Incantations that make you stronger

In a previous chapter, I said I'd share some incantations with you.

Be open-minded about the concept and be positive. Be like a sponge that's *open and willing to absorb the good stuff* and not like a closed door that's shut and not willing to open up to new ideas. Speak them out loud, with emotion, get your body involved and move with them! Jump, punch the air, dance. Let's get some motion and build the emotion!

> I love my life and I am blessed.

> Love flows through me.

Put a different emphasis on a simple phrase to make it mean more to you, such as a cultural or religious approach.

I used to think that 'perfect' was the only way to be, but now I know that all I need is here inside of me.

I appreciate and honour myself and when push comes to shove, all I ever have to do is add a little bit of love.

This one is for you if you're super-motivated!

Every day in every way I feel better and better. Yes

Every day in every way I feel stronger and stronger. Yes

Every day in every way I feel happier and happier. Yes

Every day in every way I feel more abundant. Yes

This is really simple, and you can substitute the emotional words to ones that mean more to you.

All I need is within me now

All ***I*** need is within me now

All I ***need*** is within me now

All I need ***is*** within me now

All I need is ***within*** me now

All I need is within ***me*** now

All I need is within me ***now***

Emphasising different words in each sentence combined with repetition makes this incantation hugely powerful.

Say an incantation with feeling and movement for five minutes when you're in the shower, out running, walking to or from school, at home in your bedroom – wherever works for you. Very quickly incantations can reprogramme your neural network and discourage negative thinking and behaviours.

Incantations will change your energy and rewire your thoughts.

"Dream the impossible. Seek the unknown. Achieve greatness."

Unknown

Chapter 19

How to master self-worth so that resilience falls into place

"Strong people have a strong sense of self-worth and self-awareness; they don't need the approval of others."

Roy T Bennett

You may be in a place in your life where you don't feel super confident about the future or you're a little unsure about how the decisions you make now will impact your adult self. Hopefully, this book has helped, and the practical exercises have enabled you to start building resilience and ease out negative thoughts.

Change will happen and it's OK to feel uncertain

A big lesson to share with you is that even most successful adults understand the feeling of uncertainty. The decisions you make now can always be changed and it's never too late to take a step in a different direction. Life is a learning experience that never stops, and your journey will have ups and downs, exactly as it will have left turns, right turns and even a few turns that point backwards for a period. But it's more than OK.

What is important is the concept of SELF-WORTH and giving yourself the respect you deserve. Respect how you feel, take pride in your decisions and chase those dreams so that you have every possible chance to make them reality. You may be young, but you are your own person. Grasp your dreams and aspirations with both hands and build your self-worth.

Value yourself

If you value yourself it will feel like you've found a cloak of confidence. This extra layer of protection shrouds you with a coolness, certainty and satisfaction in the decisions you make. Self-worth will allow you to strip away the "Am I good enough?" questions that bring self-doubt and cause you to compare yourself to others. *You are good enough.* You always have been and always will be – *think about resilient thinking.*

Teen pressures will test your resilience, and challenge your thoughts and opinions, but you must learn to trust your gut instinct. If others gnaw away at your ideas or scoff at your beliefs, just maybe they aren't the type of people to be your friends – *think about effective relationships.*

Trust in yourself

If you feel a lack of confidence in your abilities or have insecurities about body image, you may have listened to other people's negative opinions or been subjected to bullying or some form of humiliation. Believing hurtful comments will knock your confidence and you may feel judged by others as inadequate. What tends to happen is that you repeat a situation or comment over and over until you start to believe it. In some cases, coping mechanisms – such as self-harm, substance abuse or becoming withdrawn from friends and family – may develop; *think about managing emotions.*

Please, please understand that this is not your behaviour or belief system, but someone else's, and they are the ones in the wrong. You are worth so much more, so never let the opinions of others or spiteful comments weigh you down in a negative way. It can spiral out of control.

The great news is that self-worth will enable you to grow strong and rise above it all, so go you! Have faith in yourself, acknowledge and nurture your strengths and abilities. Picture yourself rising above it and being the achiever, despite the sceptics. Let go of doubt, release any feelings of humiliation and never hold on to anger – *think about building strength.*

Empower yourself with self-worth

Follow these three simple steps to gain a newfound self-worth. You own this!

1. Speak about what you admire

For the next seven days (or longer), tell three people (or more) – friends, family, teachers, work colleagues – something that you admire or appreciate about them. What is it that you like about them and why do you enjoy spending time with them? Be honest and open.

An example could be, "I just want to let you know that I really appreciate you helping me with my maths homework today. I was really struggling with it and you were kind to help me." Or, "Thanks ever so much for hanging out tonight – I really enjoyed it. Thanks for being a great friend." Or, "I love your sense of humour; you make me chuckle out loud so much and I really love that about you, thank you!"

You feel a bit nervous doing this at first, but I promise you it gets easier the more you do it and you will feel great as soon as the words leave your mouth. But why would you do this?

Because when you see something in someone that you admire, it's like looking in a mirror, it's a reflection of what is within you.

It will seem humbling to you, but the other person will feel tremendous, even if they don't show it. You have added value to their world and given their self-worth a top-up. And what goes around comes around, right?

2. Notice the compliments you receive

Let's get one thing straight: you will have received many compliments before, but if your self-worth wasn't brimming, you will probably have shrugged them off with "It's nothing" or "Thanks, it wasn't that good" or even a "Yeah, but XYZ was so much better." The last comment is choosing to compare yourself with others, and by doing this, you'll undervalue your true worth.

From today, notice the positive things people say to you and accept compliments as true of your skills and personality. I want you to say two words in response: "Thank you." Don't get big-headed. Instead, agree with the compliment, let it fill up your self-esteem, store it and reflect on it later. Also smile ☺. It takes fewer muscles to smile than it does to frown and it's also infectious and good for you – try it!

Practise, practise, practise. After seven days, it'll start to become natural and you'll want to praise people and smile, even at strangers.

3. Five things that are great about you

Finally, write down five things that you like about yourself. Start each thing with a phrase like "I love being me because …". A good place to start is to think about the compliments you've received. These qualities must be about you as a person and not achievements such as being head boy or head girl at school, or the latest swimming certificate. You must also have some evidence as to why it's a good quality.

Some examples might be "I love being me because I'm caring; I took care of my little sister when she fell and grazed her knee this morning" or "I like being me because I'm thoughtful; this afternoon I made my mum a cup of tea when she hadn't even asked for one", and so on.

Do this for the next 10 days, a new set of five things every day, and you'll be amazed at how many great attributes you come up with. At the end of the 10 days, you'll have 50 reasons why you're such a wonderful person.

See, I said you were amazing! You'll be glowing inside, and your self-worth will be overflowing.

When you know who you are at your core, you become unshakeable.

"Sticks and stones may break my bones, but names can never hurt me." You must have heard this saying. And it's so true, because once you know your self-worth and have your list of how amazing you are, when someone says something about you that in the past would have been hurtful, you can just say, "Wait a moment, let me check my list. NO! That's not who I am. Sorry, that's just your opinion!" You can then easily allow the words to bounce right off your new resilient self.

"Be yourself, everyone else is already taken."

Oscar Wilde

Chapter 20

Are you getting enough sleep?

"Sleep is the golden chain that ties health and our bodies together."

Thomas Dekker

On a scale of one to 10, with one being not nearly enough and 10 being plenty, how much sleep are you getting?

It might seem like an unnecessary question because you're young and (supposedly) full of energy. Insufficient sleep will, however, impact your daily life and your mental and physical wellbeing because you won't perform at an optimal level and look or feel your best.

The power of sleep is massively underrated.

Understanding how much sleep you need, along with the advantages and disadvantages of quality time in your pit, will help you to gain more energy and excel at school, at work and at leisure.

Exactly how much sleep do teenagers need?

Lots!

You might feel a little resistant towards this statement. There's something rebellious about staying up late or sleeping in and you're probably thinking, "What's the big deal?" or "It's cool to stay up late and I'm not a kid anymore." Well, *sleep requirements and patterns shift massively during your teenage years*, so it's useful to know what you're dealing with. Plus, it's scientifically proven.

- 9 to 12-year-olds need 9–12 hours' sleep every night

- Teenagers (13–17) need 8–10 hours' sleep every night

- 18 to 25-year-olds need 7–11 hours' sleep every night

Where do you fit in?

The recommended number of hours needed per night doesn't mean that eight hours for a teen every night is enough. Eight hours is the absolute minimum and 10 is ideal.

Find your ideal sleeping pattern

In your teenage years, your body clock shifts and it's true that you don't feel as tired as early. While this makes it OK to go to bed later, it doesn't make it OK to sit glued to a mobile device or become enthralled in a movie or game at midnight. Participating in this type of activity will compound the effects of not wanting to go to sleep. The blue light emitted from mobile devices also affects your sleep quality, so they need to be avoided for at least half an hour before you go to bed.

Work back from when you need to get up in the morning. If you need to be up by 7am, you need to go to sleep by 11pm at the very latest. If this is a weekly routine because of school, college or university, try to get at least two nights of 10 hours' sleep over the weekend and top up with an afternoon nap. Be aware though that too much sleep will have the opposite effect and make you feel worse – like having a sleep hangover.

Bright and breezy or groggy as hell

Tossing and turning in bed, feeling like you've not slept a wink is awful. What's even more annoying is when you wake up thinking you've had loads of sleep, but you feel shattered. Urgh!

Understanding your sleep cycle can help you improve your quality of sleep. Using a sleep app will track your sleeping pattern and provide insightful data about the quality of your sleep. Over time you'll get an indication as to what a good night's sleep looks like for you. Remember, consistency is everything.

Check out the following apps:

- **For tracking sleep**
  - o Sleep Cycle: www.sleepcycle.com
  - o Pillow:
    www.neybox.com/pillow-sleep-tracker-en
- **For helping you fall asleep**
  - o Pzizz: www.pzizz.com
  - o Insight Timer: www.insighttimer.com
- **For snorers**
  - o SnoreLab: www.snorelab.com

Sleep is for wimps!

I used to think that sleep was for wimps too. I've always led a busy life and my time in bed ranged from four to six hours. With age, I've realised how important sleep is for a healthy body and mind, so I've upped my hours in the sack. Power naps are also valuable and there's scientific evidence to suggest that they *boost your energy*.

Check out *When* by Daniel Pink – www.danpink.com – a book that considers the best timing of things. He calls naps 'nappichinos' because, apparently, a quick coffee before a 20-minute power nap is the perfect time for the caffeine to kick in. Double energy boost!

The disadvantage of limited sleep

As if changing hormones messing up your moods weren't enough, poor sleeping patterns magnify this. Your body uses sleep to rest, reset, repair and build new habits. It's vital that your body can develop and function properly. If not, problems arise, and you can become:

- Irritable
- Forgetful
- Aggressive
- Emotional
- Impatient
- Anxious
- Lethargic

Sleep deprivation stops you being able to think clearly and process information. You could find it difficult to listen, learn and concentrate on anything, not just tricky concepts presented by teachers, parents and managers.

The health disadvantages of limited sleep

Sleep deficiency can make you prone to spots and weight gain. You may find that you crave sugary or fatty foods and have an increased appetite. The knock-on effect of these physical symptoms is a dip in your self-confidence and self-worth, which are mental health issues. Your mood will be affected by poor sleep habits and you will have low energy levels and feel drowsy.

Insufficient sleep can also heighten the effects of caffeine, energy drinks and alcohol, causing an increase in heart rate and blood pressure. More importantly, it will affect your body's immune system because there isn't time to heal properly. As a result, you are likely to be more prone to coughs, colds, tummy troubles and migraines.

Furthermore, many studies show the detrimental effects of sustained sleep deficiency being contributory factors in the development of critical illnesses. This book isn't about scaremongering. As you are still young, your body is better equipped to fight off infection so severe issues will only manifest after *prolonged sleep deprivation or* due to other underlying illnesses, but that's not an excuse to stay up late. The bottom line is: get plenty of sleep!

Discover the benefits of superb sleep

You want to be a healthy, pimple-free, lean machine and have the ability to achieve what you want. Work towards this by developing a sleep routine that works for you, so you can see and feel the benefits.

Try this exercise for the next 10 days to make sleep a priority. Keep a diary or journal to make a note of the changes: what works and what doesn't. Follow these steps.

- Turn your bedroom into a sleep haven – cool, quiet and dark.

- Use an eye mask or hang up black-out curtains if needed.

- Avoid caffeine, alcohol and eating at least an hour before bedtime.

- Keep a journal by your bedside and jot down any thoughts before you sleep to empty your mind.

- Wake up to natural sunlight – it helps.

- Be consistent in your sleep habits to gain a natural rhythm.

- Make notes on how you feel the next morning, after a week and 10 days. Try to understand the reasons why you have a good or bad night's sleep to learn best practices.

Establish a routine of having a bedtime and waking-up time that works for you. And when you hear your mates speak of late-night parties and gaming until the early hours, tell them how cool it is to get a good night's kip.

"Happiness consists of getting enough sleep. Just that, nothing more."

Robert A Heinlein

Chapter 21

Full of empty pizza, pasta and chocolate?

"Keep your vitality. A life without health is like a river without water."

Maxime Lagacé

Supporting your body and mind to feel your best

You will always have tough decisions to make in life. Right now, you may be considering academic changes or making career choices that will take you on to higher education or dipping your toe in the job market.

First of all, let me wish you the best of luck with your decisions. Second, let me share two key elements that will improve your mental health and wellbeing to best support your body and mind through making challenging decisions. They will support your resilience.

These two factors are HYDRATION *and* NUTRITION. It seems simple and powerful, but it frustrates me to see how so many people fail to grasp the true benefit of drinking water and eating nutritious food.

Finding your fuel and feeding your mind and body

You have a natural FUEL that helps you to stay in tune with your mind and body. We'll discuss this more in the next chapter. The right fuel will allow you to be your best because you are being your authentic self and living in the zone. *When you are in the zone you cannot feel stressed, depressed or anxious.* The natural gifts and talents that you excel at fuel the energy in your body so that you can live life (relatively) effortlessly. But if you want to find this fuel and live well, your body needs to be supported and nurtured. Let me share how you can do this.

Are you too acidic?

Now, if you're wondering where this is going and you don't want to read a scientific essay, it's OK, I won't get too technical, but I do need to stress the importance of keeping your body in an alkaline state with plenty of water and clean food. In fact, your blood needs to be alkaline, with a pH of 7.362 to be precise. Just for reference, the pH scale is a measure of how much acid is present in something.

Your clever body has developed ways to keep your pH levels spot on, yet day in, day out consuming pizza, chocolate, chips and energy drinks becomes the norm. Aren't all those foods part of a typical teenage diet? Think about it for a minute: if you were to put sugar in the fuel tank of a car, how far would it get? It may go for a short while, but soon it would cough, splutter and eventually conk out. And that is exactly what will happen to your body if you persist with a poor diet or, worse still, substance abuse. Sugar, coffee, energy drinks and drugs provide a short-term high. Without the kick of the high you feel low and lethargic, with no mental drive or physical energy.

Do you feel lethargic?

If you feel sluggish, it might be because you've binged on pizza, popcorn, sweets and fizzy drinks. Too much sugar and fat in your body acts like glue in your blood. This overindulgence slows your blood flow and results in fewer nutrients and less oxygen reaching the vital organs in your body. Fast foods, convenience foods and sweet, fatty foods rob you of your energy. They affect your skin, your weight, your confidence and more, causing things such as:

- Upset stomach
- Acne
- Migraines
- Blood pressure issues
- Immune system problems

How much is poor diet affecting your confidence and self-worth? How do you react if you're not feeling and looking your best?

Make better choices with your food and see how different you feel.

Create an alkaline body

Your body is super-clever. Let me ask you a question. How much water do you drink? I'm not talking about tea, coffee, fizzy drinks, or a cheeky beer or gin. I'm talking about water and ideally two litres of the clear stuff every day. Water flushes acids and toxins from your body, which in turn supports your blood to stay alkaline. But what happens if you don't drink enough water to aid this flushing process?

To counteract the lack of water, your body will transfer acids into the fat reserves of your body. If you are struggling with weight gain, it may be that you are 'over-acid' rather than overweight. Worryingly, if this process continues there will come a point when there are no more fat cells available to contain the acid so your body will start to buffer the toxin by leaching calcium from your bones and teeth. Why do you think athletes such as long-distance runners suffer from bone disorders? It's because they have a constant build-up of lactic acid and their super-clever bodies filter the calcium as a form of protection.

Fast-forward further and once the calcium is depleted, your body will start to overproduce cholesterol as a protection measure. The cholesterol is deposited in your blood stream and around vital organs to protect them against the acid. Can you picture this? Your organs and arteries furred up with cholesterol. Urgh!

Can you see how this spiralling process will inevitably lead to complications? There are so many poor health knock-on effects due to lack of hydration and bad food choices. Is it worth it? Go and pour a glass of the clear stuff and make a green salad right now ☺.

Feel your best through good nutrition and hydration

When you support your body by keeping it hydrated and consuming clean foods, you have more energy and feel more alert. You can make decisions with clarity and handle challenging situations more easily, simply because you are healthier in mind and body. It's so simple.

Challenge your diet

I guarantee that if you change your diet to eat real food instead of man-made food for at least *70 per cent of the time,* your mental and physical energy will skyrocket. You'll be amazed at how well you feel in yourself because your brain is fuelled in the right way.

Keep a food and drink diary for a week. Make a note of the times you eat and drink and what you consume. Include how the food was prepared and the method of cooking. After each meal or snack, grade how full you feel and your energy level, on a scale of one to 10. Note also how you feel at night and first thing in the morning – is there a pattern based on what you ate and how much water you drank? A really cool way to notice any trends is to keep a daily food diary.

I'm not saying that you should ditch the chocolate or pizza: just keep them to a minimum. Your future self will thank you for it.

"Let food be thy medicine and medicine be thy food."

Hippocrates

Chapter 22

Ease your teenage stresses by mastering the magic of now

> *"Mindfulness is a way of befriending ourselves and our experience."*

Jon Kabat-Zinn

Allow me to introduce the *'magic of now'* as a solution to ease your teenage stresses. "What the …?" I hear you mumble. Don't panic, I'm not going to make you delve into the world of Harry Potter to create spells or discuss anything mathematical that's going to tax your brain. Instead, I want to introduce you to a simple method that you can call on when you feel a bit fed up, sad or grouchy, to help you to relax and feel more like yourself again. It'll also give you an energy boost without the sugar!

As difficult as it might sound, be in the moment

When was the last time you felt chilled out and thoroughly in tune with what you were doing? It can be difficult to *be in the moment* because so often you think about the past or worry about the future, and as a tween, teen or even in your early 20s there's so much going on. With so much new stuff being thrown your way and even more new decisions to make, life can feel like a never-ending rollercoaster loop.

Think carefully: where were you when you last felt truly happy and content? Would you like to feel happy like this more often?

How valuable would it be to know how to step away from overwhelming feelings, to let go of anxieties and take stress in your stride? Your answer is MINDFULNESS.

Mindfulness is right here, right now

Mindfulness is all about living 100 per cent in the present moment without getting caught up with the pains of the past or fears of the future.

There's no point worrying about finding the perfect career path, the ideal partner or lifetime holiday. It will happen when it happens, and it will be amazing. There's no point reliving the disappointment of a failed exam, the pain of an accident or the embarrassment of a mishap. They have happened and you can't change that.

Focus on the 'now'

Notice what's happening around you. It might even put a smile on your face. Mindfulness isn't difficult. You don't have to be sitting cross-legged on a mountain in Asia (the stereotypical vision of a monk practising meditation). You can be mindful anywhere, no matter what you're doing and once you've experienced it and practised it, it can become your go-to de-stresser. Say goodbye to binge chocolate feasts, box sets or wanting to be alone to make you feel better. Mindfulness is the future.

Why is mindfulness good for teenagers?

Well, it's not just good for teenagers, it's great for everyone, but people often think it's something that only older people practise.

Meditation is a practice of mindfulness, and has wonderful results. It's easy because it's just breathing. The heart of mindfulness is your breath. And breath is a wonderful thing because it brings more oxygen into your body, helps you to absorb more nutrients and gets rid of yucky toxins that shouldn't be there. Breath helps calm your chatty mind and free your thoughts from the pains of the past and fears of the future.

Meditation doesn't have to be for long and you can practise it pretty much anywhere. Plus, it has many benefits, such as:

- Lowering blood pressure
- Reducing stress
- Getting oxygen to the brain for calm thinking
- Reducing toxin build-up
- Reducing carbon dioxide
- Boosting the immune system
- Improving one's sense of wellbeing
- Releasing healthy neurotransmitters – healing for both your mind and body.

There is evidence that people who meditate look younger because they are more relaxed. And they have fewer wrinkles. You won't have to worry about that yet, but I'm all for it at my age.

You can read more here: www.theguardian.com/science/blog/2016/mar/03/could-meditation-really-help-slow-the-ageing-process

Focus on your breathing — breath meditation

Let's try this now; there's no time like the present.

You may prefer to listen to a podcast if it's easier. If so, visit the link below and start at 11:10. You don't have to close your eyes so there's no need to worry that people might think you're weird.

https://shows.acast.com/sparktoyoursuccess/episodes/the-magic-of-now

Bring your attention to your breath. Don't make it any different; it doesn't need to be slower or deeper. Notice the mood and air as you inhale oxygen and breathe out carbon dioxide. You can experiment and choose words to say to yourself when breathing in and out. Words denoting emotions — such as breathing in calmness and breathing out tension – are good. Say an affirmation when you breathe in, such as, *"My world is good, my life is good,"* or *"I am good."*

Follow your breath's journey, down into the lungs and out again. Notice the pause at the end. Notice how your body feels. Notice your chest rise as you breathe in and fall as you breathe out. Notice the air coming in through your nostrils then leaving through your mouth. This shouldn't have to feel like work: it's only natural. Feel yourself relaxing. Smile to tell your face you're enjoying it.

Allow random thoughts to creep in – it's OK

If you notice thoughts popping into your head or you think you've drifted off, that's fine. Just catch them and don't judge yourself in any way. Let the thoughts go and come back to your breath.

Mindfulness takes practice, but you can experience the relaxation from as little as three breaths. Let's do three together now. Again, if you would prefer to listen to a podcast spoken guide, visit the link below and go to 15:48.

https://shows.acast.com/sparktoyoursuccess/episodes/the-magic-of-now

Say whatever you want to yourself as you breathe in and out. Let's go:

- Breathe in.
- Hold for a moment.
- Breathe out.
- Notice the end.

And again:

- Breathe in calm.
- Hold for a moment.
- Breathe out stress and tension.
- Notice the end.

And finally:

- Breathe in and feel yourself relax.

- Hold for a moment.

- Breathe out and let any worries escape with your breath.

- Notice the end.

How do you feel after just three breaths?

Explore different ways to meditate

Choose a place and a time where you have at least 20 minutes to practise meditating. Your room might be a good place, as it's a private space, or maybe a quiet woodland area if it's warm outside. I would suggest trying a few different practices over a few days to see what works best.

- **No-thought meditation**
  - o This is exactly as it sounds – relax and think of nothing. Focus on one object in your room, such as a candle or picture, as this can keep your inner voice at bay.

- **Mantra meditation**
  - o Pick a meaningful phrase and repeat it over and over and in different ways, emphasising certain words.

- **Breath meditation**
  - o Concentrate and follow your breathing, taking deep breaths in and out.

- **Sound meditation**
  - o Relax to chill-out music designed specifically to aid meditation as you focus on a topic or challenge.

- **Visual meditation**
  - o Picture the past or present or imagine the future and concentrate your efforts on letting something go or making something a reality.

- **Gratitude meditation**
  - o Deeply contemplate something you feel grateful for – feel and visualise it and be thankful.

- **Guided meditation**
  - o Listen to a trained professional talk you through a meditation practice.

For guided meditation try listening to:

Deepak Chopra: www.deepakchopra.com

Dr Wayne Dyer: www.drwaynedyer.com

Dr Joe Dispenza: www.drjoedispenza.com

When you meditate, it changes your state of mind because your thoughts are focused on what you are doing. Discover what method and time of day is best for your routine.

"If you want to conquer the anxiety of life, live in the moment, live in the breath."

Amit Ray

Chapter 23

What does your flow look like?

"Energy flows where intention goes."

Rhonda Byrne

The word 'FLOW' might sound a bit soft and woolly, but I promise you it's not. Flow is one of the most important elements for you to discover in life. Ponder this word for a moment; what does flow mean to you?

Do you think of it as 'going with the flow', 'going your own way', being 'in the zone', feeling as though 'things are easy' or does it perhaps raise images in your mind such as 'water'? Well, flow is all those things and so much more. Flow is not a somebody or a thing: it's a 'state of being'.

Exploring your flow

FLOW is the place you find yourself when it's *challenging but not overstretching*. It's a state of mind, whatever you are doing or feeling, that's enough for it not to be boring. It is a great place to be when you're involved in something you enjoy yet you're being challenged on some level – in a good way. Being in flow will usually apply to your natural gifts and talents, and it's a great skill to be able to *align yourself to your flow.*

Imagine the flow of a river. It starts as a trickle and grows in volume. It's a force of nature that has a purpose. A stream may grow to a river and it naturally flow into a lake or the sea. There are obstacles in the river's path, such as boulders or trees, but it always overcomes them by finding a way to go over, under or around them. Well, that's what it's like to be in flow. *You have found your purpose and you will overcome all obstacles.*

This Lucozade flow video captures the notion perfectly and its slogan, "The unmistakable feeling of being unstoppable," is bang on. What do you think?

Please do watch it and share your thoughts on social media: https://www.youtube.com/watch?v=CCElBu7tNAY

- www.instagram.com/ignition.rocks

- www.facebook.com/IgnitionYP

- www.twitter.com/ignition2017

Why you should be in flow

When you are in flow, you cannot feel stressed, depressed or anxious. Being in flow helps to remove mental health challenges, the immense pressures of exams, puberty and just general teen angst – or at least it equips you with the appropriate and positive mental state for you to take them in your stride.

Picture the scene: you're at home and your mum or dad has been calling you for tea (for ages, they said), but you haven't heard a thing? That's because you were completely in the zone, 100 per cent feeling your flow, and time has a habit of disappearing when you are enjoying yourself.

When you're in flow, you have more energy and feel exhilarated. You are motivated and have a sense of anticipation, even a mix of nerves and excitement. When you're in flow it's because you are doing something that you're naturally good at and it doesn't take much of an effort. It gives you energy and a feeling of being alive. A learned behaviour or skill, on the other hand, or something that doesn't come naturally for you, takes energy and effort and can have the opposite effect and put you out of flow.

Are you in flow now?

Where would you put yourself right now, as you read this, on a scale of 1–10 (1 being pretty pooped and 10 being amazing) in terms of how your flow feels? You might have a different scale of 1–10 at home, at school or when you're with friends and family. How incredible would the difference be if you hitched up the score by a notch or two? This is where your resilience comes in. Thinking in a resilient way, spending time only on positive relationships, managing your emotions effectively and building strengths helps you to find your flow and keeps you there.

Here's how to find your flow

What does flow look like for you and what elements are in flow for you each day?

Could it be your imagination? Are you expressive? How do the following activities make you feel?

- Creative writing

- Playing an instrument

- Singing or dancing

- Being an adrenaline junkie

- Crafting

The more creative you are, the less anxious you'll be.

Perhaps you enjoy more analytical and theoretical activities:

- Researching

- Planning

- Solving problems

- Getting enthralled in a deep conversation

- Reading poetry

- Listening to music

You may prefer to be a social bunny or enjoy quiet time on your own.

Try the following exercise and revisit it every few weeks to see what changes take place.

Write down three or four things in each part of your life – such as school, friends, family, work and hobbies – and think about the following in terms of when it feels easy, natural or enjoyable.

- Which activities do you enjoy?

- Which day is best?

- Which time of day is best?

- Who do you prefer to be with at the time?

- Which factors improve the outcome?

- Which factors spoil the outcome?

- How could you make it even better?

Ultimately being in flow makes you happy. If you're not happy or not in flow, the task at hand can feel exhausting. This is because it takes more of your energy to participate in or complete it. You may have something that you keep pushing to the bottom of the list or ignoring, hoping it will go away. It's stressful and frustrating. But honestly, because you still need to do it, unless you can pass it on, take a deep breath and jump straight in. Look at it this way: the quicker you do it, the quicker you can move on to something you do enjoy, and your flow will return.

Identify the things that feel demanding on your time or skills and make you feel anxious. Jot these down too as opposites to the things you enjoy. Once you recognise the difference, it's easier for you to choose what to do with them.

Fuel your 'flow' and start your journey to success

You are in control of your own destiny and it *is* possible to rise above the daily pressures you face as a teenager, by tackling them with a positive frame of mind.

Think about when you jump into the car with family or friends, about to embark on an adventure. Maybe you're driving already – congratulations if you are and have your own wheels.

The car starts with an ignition, a mechanical process that you might not be aware of, where a spark is required to light the fuel in the engine so that it can operate. I believe that we all have a bright spark inside and when you light up your spark, not only do you light up inside, but you light up the world around you too. However, it's not the spark that takes you on your journey: the spark lights the *fuel* in your vehicle to *take* you on your journey.

This is exactly what happens in your body when you feel in 'flow'.

You must have the right fuel in your vehicle for it to be easy and effortless, but imagine this: have you ever been in a situation where petrol was pumped into a diesel car or vice versa? It's not a great outcome, is it? The car coughs and splutters, stops and starts, your vehicle is damaged and then you have a breakdown.

A similar thing happens to you if you don't find the right fuel for your flow. This is why so many people suffer from anxiety, inferiority complexes, even depression. On a simple level they are fighting with everything that doesn't come naturally to them. We have too many young people having a breakdown because they don't know about flow and as a result are out of flow.

Finding the right fuel for your flow

Flow is not a new concept: it has thousands of years of successful history. The ancient Chinese called it 'spirit energy' and they were using it back in ninth century BC in the I Ching or Yi Jing manuscript. If you are interested, this has been translated and adapted into a modern English book called I Ching or Book of Changes: www.amazon.co.uk/I-Ching-Book-Changes-Arkana/dp/0140192077

I encourage you to look up the work of Mihaly Csikszentmihalyi, who wrote a book about flow. You can also find him on TED Talks.

www.pursuit-of-happiness.org/history-of-happiness/mihaly-csikszentmihalyi

www.ted.com/talks/mihaly_csikszentmihalyi_on_flow

Another great believer in the concept of flow is psychologist Gay Hendricks, who wrote a book called *The Big Leap*: www.harpercollins.co.uk/9780061735363/the-big-leap-conquer-your-hidden-fear-and-take-life-to-the-next-level

There are four main fuels and often you will find that you are a mix of two. Everyone is different. There is no wrong or right and no better or worse. Let's find your fuel.

"Life is like a river. The way of life is to flow with the current. To turn against it takes effort but the current will carry you if you let it. Float with joy and ease."

Anonymous

Chapter 24

Finding the fuel that makes you magnificent

"If you fuel your journey on the opinions of others, you are going to run out of gas."

Steve Maraboli

Finding your fuel is about *discovering your purpose* and why you do what you do.

- Why do certain activities or ideas draw you in?

- What do you enjoy?

- What don't you enjoy?

- Do you enjoy activities on your own or within a team?

- Are you a leader or a follower?

The right fuel gives you the key to understanding what you are doing and only you know what's right for you.

Discover your fuel

To find your fuel, let's start by asking five questions. The answers should come quickly, but don't worry if you have to think about them. Most people have a dominant fuel, but two can be closely linked, so if you feel as though you're torn between two answers, label one of them a one and the other a two.

Which of these do you enjoy doing MOST?

1. Spending time by yourself.

2. Going out and meeting new people.

3. Using your imagination and ideas to create things.

4. Taking care of other people and ensuring they feel valued.

Which of these do you enjoy the LEAST?

1. Having to go out and meet a lot of people you don't know.

2. Having to explain things in detail to people.

3. Looking at data on spreadsheets.

4. Coming up with new plans and ideas.

Which of these do you find the EASIEST?

1. Organising the details, data and systems.

2. Starting new things.

3. Finding bargains.

4. Getting on with people.

Which of these do you find the MOST DIFFICULT?

1. Reading detailed instruction manuals.

2. Being entertaining to strangers.

3. Patiently waiting for answers.

4. Coming up with great ideas quickly.

When deciding to buy something, do you:

1. Picture yourself using or wearing it?

2. Ask other people's thoughts about the product?

3. Do your research to find out all the options?

4. Use your gut feeling about it, as long as it's the right price?

We'll come to the answers in the next chapter, so please don't be tempted to take a peek. Be strong and hold back the urge ☺.

Fuel your day, week and future ahead

Life is so much better when you feel happy in your own skin, when you enjoy what you're doing, and you feel supported with those you spend time with. There are so many enriching experiences waiting for you to join in and understanding what your fuel is will open up opportunities for you.

You are in control of your own destiny, as I've said many times throughout this book, and it is possible to rise above the daily pressures facing you as a teenager by tackling them with a positive frame of mind.

This is why I developed the Ignition! programme. It's designed to empower young people, just like you, to build confidence and boost self-worth, and to provide you with a vision and direction when making decisions for your future ahead and career ideas.

It doesn't matter where your life began, how your life has unfolded so far, or where you currently are. It matters that you discover who you are. Not your name or your labels, but who you really are. It matters that you identify what you are naturally gifted and talented at. It also matters that you acknowledge what you are naturally not so good at.

Discovering the fuel that gives your life energy and meaning will keep you in flow for the *rest* of your life.

Let's check out what fuel you need to become magnificent.

"A person's passion is the fuel that drives their purpose."

Laurie Buchanan

Chapter 25

Where does your fuel point? Where do you get your gas?

"Abundance is a flow of energy through you."

Steve Rother

It's important to appreciate what your natural gifts are and the type of fuel that gives you your flow, as this will help you to live a more fulfilled life.

It's equally important to recognise that *your greatest qualities may be someone else's worst.* This is why people with different fuels often complement each other, but also why some people conflict.

Being able to identify and appreciate this is a powerful skill, so it's worth putting in a bit of time and effort.

Below are the four main fuels. Read through each one because you will have one main fuel, but you may notice characteristics in friends, family members, even enemies (meant in the nicest possible way), that will help you to understand them better.

Fuel 1: NOVA – north point on the compass

If Nova were a season, it would be springtime because it's a fast-paced fuel, full of life. People who thrive on Nova fuel have lots of ideas and a creative imagination, and they love to invent or innovate.

If this sounds familiar, you are spontaneous but not the best at timing. You may change your mind often and find yourself deviating from plans, but you are a big picture thinker. You always look on the bright side, but sometimes you think you can achieve more than you can in the given time. You are an inspiration to those around you and you love to get new things started. You may not necessarily get these same things finished as the novelty wears off if progress takes too long and you lose the inspiration. You can be impatient with yourself and others and consequently you find it difficult to pass on responsibility. You have high expectations and can be disappointed easily.

Sound familiar? If not, who is close to you who has these traits?

Fuel 2: EXUBERANT — east point on the compass

Exuberant fuel as a season would be summer because this fuel creates warmth, friendliness and passion. It can also be a bit fiery.

Are you energised by friends and family, and love to be around people – lots of people? If so, Exuberant could be your fuel. You love to get stuck in and connect with as many people as possible. You may well talk more than you listen (which can be noticed). You take energy from outside and bring it inside, as you love variety in your life and constantly ask questions because you're curious and are like a sponge when it comes to dipping your toe in.

Being a social butterfly, you love a party and are great at spotting the potential in those around you and nurturing them by saying so. You're competitive and love being in a team, so an open plan office or large organisation would be perfect for you to work in. You often seek the opinions of others before making your own decision, because you value feedback just so long as you don't get confused.

Can you relate to these behaviours? If not, can you recognise them in a friend or family member?

Fuel 3: SENSATIONAL – south point on the compass

Sensational as a season would be autumn, and as an element, earth, because it's a grounding fuel.

If this is you, you are good at sensing the world around you, in nature and in people as you use your senses – touch, taste, hear, see and smell – to your advantage. You instinctively know the right time to do something and have strong gut feelings. You have deep thoughts, are caring and want to look after people, animals or the environment. You'll always go the extra mile, but you can be upset easily because you're sensitive and overthink situations, taking throwaway comments to heart. You like things to be fair and you are good at planning and will always make sure the job gets done by the right people and at the right time – but you'll want proof of a positive outcome before you take action.

Do any of these characteristics resonate with you? Perhaps they remind you of someone close?

Fuel 4: WISE – west point on the compass

The Wise fuel is all about facts and figures, data analysis and structure. If this sounds familiar, you may not be a 'people person' because you want to get stuck into the finer detail, dot the Is and cross the Ts, and do your research to find all the facts. You don't need validation from other people to get the job done and you are brilliant at taking control and bringing certainty to a situation. You do also need a lot of certainty and want to know the steps to follow for the project, the agenda for the meeting or the itinerary for the trip.

Being in a social setting for long periods doesn't come naturally to you and it saps your energy. Your patience can run thin and you want people to get to the point quickly because you just need the stark facts – idle chitchat is not for you. It's not that you're a social recluse or that you don't like being around people: it's just that quiet time alone helps you to replenish your energy levels.

As a season, Wise would be winter.

How relatable are these behaviours to you? Does it sound like someone in your circle or friends or family?

Choose your fuel

So which fuel are you? Have you decided after reading the main characteristics of each fuel? Review your choice from the last chapter below to see if it confirms your feelings.

Which of these do you enjoy doing MOST?

W – Spending time by yourself.

E – Going out and meeting new people.

N – Using your imagination and ideas to create things.

S – Taking care of other people and ensuring they feel valued.

Which of these do you enjoy the LEAST?

W – Having to go out and meet a lot of people you don't know.

N – to explain things in detail to people.

S – Looking at data on spreadsheets.

E – Coming up with new plans and ideas.

Which of these do you find the EASIEST?

W – Organising the details, data and systems.

N – Starting new things.

S – Finding bargains.

E – Getting on with people.

Which of these do you find the MOST DIFFICULT?

E – Reading detailed instruction manuals.

W – Being entertaining to strangers.

N – Patiently waiting for answers.

S – Coming up with great ideas quickly.

When deciding to buy something, do you:

N – Picture yourself using or wearing it?

E – Ask other people's thoughts about the product?

W – Do your research to find out all the options?

S – Use your gut feeling about it as long as it's the right price?

Which one came out on top for you? Or were you an equal mix of two? Once you know your ideal fuel, think about which activities and ideas will support your fuel and where you can seek more of them.

Boom – you're in flow, congratulations

Remember, you have a dominant fuel and it's common to experience traits from all fuels depending on the situation you are in. I'll throw a cautionary note in here to make you even more aware of your awesomeness: you can take on the characteristic of any fuel should you need to, depending on the situation.

The consequences of you taking on a fuel that doesn't come naturally are uncertainty, anxiety, stress and worry. This makes perfect sense because you are out of your comfort zone and out of flow. It squeezes the energy out of you and your spark wilts, but it's not permanent so don't worry. As you build your resilience, you'll get over it quickly and you'll be back in flow in no time.

Find your fuel. Get the spark to your success. Become magnificent.

"Those who flow as life flows know they need no other force."

Lao Tzu

Chapter 26

Now go be magnificent

"You are what you do, not what you say you'll do."

Carl Gustav Jung

That concludes *The Spark to Your Success: Helping Teens Build Resilience*. How do you feel?

For a young person, the pressures of modern life are immense – the academic system, social anxieties, imbalances at home and career stress. Society is hyperactive and it's difficult to see clearly.

Picture looking at yourself through a frosted window – it's ill-defined, vague, distant. Is the real you fighting to break through the fog, to gain clarity and see the beauty in life – your life? With everything you've absorbed while reading this book – the exercises, the key messages and the powerful words – you will now be on a better pathway to deal with life. You will be on your way to being and feeling magnificent.

If there's just one thing that you take away from reading this book, it's to remember that everyone is different. Everyone is shaped by past experiences, future desires, different attitudes and behaviours.

It's what makes you unique and defines your personality. No matter what, you are remarkable.

You have differences for a reason

You shouldn't be judged by the same standards and this is where the current academic system (and many pockets of society) fail young people like you. I can support you to discover your own geniuses – not those expected by teachers, parents and peers – which is why I created *Back on Track Teens* and *The Spark to Your Success* series of blogs, podcasts and books for young people, and launched the Ignition! programme.

My purpose is to empower 10 million young people to become tomorrow's confident, successful leaders, who do it by feeling happy in their own skin. I hope I've given you a little inspiration and insight and brought some positivity into your day.

Thanks for reading. I'd love to talk more, so please do share your journey with me on social media and connect with us to access even more resources to help you maintain resilience in life, achieve your inspirations and be truly magnificent.

You got this!

Always here to help

TeeJay

PS

Here's a word cloud of all the keywords we mentioned throughout the book.

PPS

Remember the exercise in chapter 8 where I asked what needs you felt were being met? Visit the link below to see how many you guessed right:

www.backontrackteens.com/needs-being-met

The resources available to you:

- www.instagram.com/ignition.rocks
- www.facebook.com/IgnitionYP
- www.twitter.com/ignition2017

- The Spark to Your Success podcast:

  https://shows.acast.com/sparktoyoursuccess

- The Spark to Your Success blog series:

  www.backontrackteens.com/blog

- Useful links and resources:

  www.backontrackteens.com/resources

If you are interested in learning more about how to support young people and want to inspire our next generation, please look up the Ignition! programme here: www.ignition.rocks/

"The future depends on what you do today."

Mahatma Gandhi

About the author

TeeJay's journey from student technician to pharmacist to neurostrategist and NLP trainer has been an amazing adventure over the last decade, and testimony to the fact that small dreams can turn into huge aspirations that even do come true!

"From the innocent age of four, I had a strong belief that I wasn't good enough. This negative emotion set me on a pathway in life where I never felt as though my face fitted – I was a loner, painfully shy and kept encountering obstacles in my career and social life.

"That belief stayed at my side for over three decades, tugging at my confidence and making life incredibly uncomfortable. Not once did anyone share the thought that I should *just be myself and believe in the real me, and that **I** was magnificent in my own unique skin.*

"I took a job instead of a career, was bullied at work, became a single parent at 19, endured a string of failed relationships, and found my escape by being emotionally numb to just get through each day. That is until LIFE intervened and gave me a wake-up call!"

Today TeeJay is the founder and CEO of Ignition! Coaching and Training and Back on Track Teens – two international self-development organisations that create partnerships with parents, youth coaches, communities and companies around the globe to maximise the transformation of a generation. She is a published author, international trainer, speaker and coach, and her purpose in life is to empower 10 million young people to become tomorrow's confident, successful leaders, by feeling happy in their own skin.